" Forgive Me
I'm a Man"

By Pip Frederick

A Pip Frederick Paperback Original 2005

Copyright (c) Pip Fredrick 2005

ISBN –10   0-9551569-0-4
ISBN –13   978-0-9551569-0-8

forgivemeimaman@hotmail.co.uk

Printed and bound in Great Britain by Express
Printing.

This book is dedicated to my daughter Samantha.
Without her I would never have written any poetry and many of the stories contained within these pages would not have happened.

She has given me purpose, responsibility, focus and reward.
As a child she was beside me through the darkest of times and the funniest of adventures.
As a woman she is the keeper of my heart and the protector of my sanity.

But most of all she is my friend.

Index of Poems

Introduction

I think for the most part, I'm just another bloke and as such have all the faults and idiosyncrasies of my species. Having now reached the age of forty-eight, I find most of the time I can control the knee-jerk reactions and mood swings which have caused so many problems for me with the opposite sex. I call them "Man Mode".

In the following pages I hope to tell you about some of the crazy and stupid things I've done and try to explain why us men find it hard to share our problems.

Why sometimes it seems easier to tell a lie than admit to fear or failure. And why a bar of chocolate threatens my masculinity.

For me the pendulum of life swings as far as it can. From Socially Responsible to Recklessly Rebellious and from Suit clad bureaucrat, to grease covered motor mechanic. I hope to take you, with the aid of my poems and anecdotes on what for me has so far been a great adventure of discovery. About both myself and those most wonderful but baffling creatures " Women".

Now I pause for a moment to give a short CV, which encapsulates my life.

Racing Cars - (Ok), Motorcycles – (Good at), Plant hire- (Ok), Lorry driver- (Great fun), Marriage- (Failed), Wind Surfing- (Good at), Dress making- (Average), Skiing- (Crap), Parent – (Not sure), Cooking- (OK), Fair ground operator- (Made money), Entertainer- (Almost made it), Circus Owner- (Look the part), Script Writer- (Tried and just made money), Coal Man – (Dirty), Friend – (loyal), Lover - (could do better), Women - (Tries hard).

It all sounds really exciting doesn't it? But the truth is, I was just trying to get by the best I could. I left school under a cloud at the age of fourteen. My size and the fact that my dad was from India, made me a shy kid, and I was so afraid of girls that I could never see when they liked me, and if I did think I had a chance, I was afraid of their rejection and would rarely go any further.
As a child I was never into Football or physical sports. I chose to play in the garden, take old TVs apart and try to build wooden go-carts.
Having spent my first decade and a half being a sad little bastard, I found Cars and Motorbikes, which changed my life dramatically.
To this day my Harley has stayed with me through several relationships, a house move, career changes, mood swings and mid-life crises. It never moans, waits patiently where I leave it, and is always ready to give me pleasure. (*Sorry that's man mode speaking*)
After my marriage failed (*like we all do*). I spent many hours thinking about what I did wrong.

Of course as you read my poems and stories I think you'll know exactly what I did wrong.
I'm a man – that should explain it all.

At that point in my life, I found myself with the responsibility of a young daughter. She wasn't dumped on me. In fact I had to fight hard to get custody of her. In all honesty I don't know if I fought through bloody mindedness or a genuine concern for her welfare. But having finally got custody and control, I knew I had to try and understand her female needs.

That was when I started talking to the women around me instead of at them, in the hope that I could understand and address the needs of this innocent child, as she grew with my guidance to be a woman. Poetry became the release from my fear of failure. With my newfound responsibilities, and the restrictions of being a one-parent family, I was afraid for most of my waking hours, but no one knew and at the time I would never admit it.

During the long nights when, I sat alone watching my daughter sleep, I was afraid of the responsibility of parenting this small and innocent child. So I wrote down the feelings in my heart, and allowed the tears that I was afraid to share with those around me, to flow onto the written page. My own words became my council, and have continued to help me to learn about myself, even to this day.

Since my early thirties I've done every thing I could to understand the culture of the female species and in doing so, come to understand my own gender better. Now more often than not I'm able to speak from the heart without fear or embarrassment, and I can take part in things traditionally reserved for women.

There is no better enjoyment for me, than to be in conversation with a group of ladies, asking questions about their views, and in return giving my male perspective. I'm often asked, " Why do men lie so much?" or " Why won't men talk about their problems?" I can only answer for myself, but I have been every type of man and I hope the one I am now is the best.

I have compiled this book using my poetry and along with anecdotes from the many occupations and hobbies I've indulged in, I hope our journey will be interesting and humorous.

My daughter would tell you that I've always surrounded myself with eccentric friends, and with one of my sayings being " You will be like the people you mix with". I guess I am a bit that way myself.

I hope the men behaving badly stories will give you a few laughs, and the darker poems a twinge of empathy. I'd like to think that if they take the time to read it, my fellow men might find the courage to admit their fears and accept the support from their partners that is so often turned away.

Whilst I am no psychologist, councillor, or oracle, I hope that my female readers will get some small insight into the hearts and minds of the male species, and I say both for myself and on behalf of all of my gender. Feel free to laugh at me, or with me.

Be angry with me or find empathy for me. But I implore you.

Please "Forgive Me I'm a Man".

Tuesday

Lying on a sun drenched beach, with
lapping Waves around my feet.
A dusky maiden by my side.
My friend, my slave, perhaps my bride.
I'm not sure what she's doing there but
as we touch I don't much care.
A coconut is in my hand; we share its
milk whilst on the sand.

THEN

Just as things are getting hot. I hear a
noise, which makes me stop.
Suddenly my maidens gone. I'm now in
bed and all alone
 The postman's been, I hear a slap, as
letters hit the front door mat.
I'll close my eyes and snuggle down
perhaps my maidens still around.

No.

Now she's gone, so I will see - What
letters lay in wait for me.

WHO CARES

I must go back into my dream. I wonder
if I can redeem the feelings found upon
that shore, to hold my maiden's hand
once more.

BUT WAIT ITS TUESDAY!

Tuesday is a special day; the winner's
cheques are on their way.
I may have won the football pools, the
premium bonds or spot the ball.

But as I check through half closed eyes.
A pile of bills has just arrived.

I wrote *Tuesday* when I was in my early thirties. I'd just been divorced and after a long and stressful legal battle had secured the custody of my daughter Sam, who was only six or seven years old. After re-mortgaging my house and paying out my ex wife. I owed twice the amount, which we had originally paid for it. Along with thousands of pounds in Council and Revenue taxes, which together with credit cards and utility bills were consuming money faster than I could earn it.

I ran a Car Repair business from my garage at home and had been working in Cabaret since the age of sixteen. Suddenly the man in me had to wake up and realise my responsibilities. Now there was a small, vulnerable child, relying on me to keep a home and care for her. I had a good family who lived very close, but as a man I felt that I couldn't show my fears and weakness to them. So the nighttimes became the escape from the threat of my creditors calling and my fantasies seemed my only hope.

During the various reports that were made about my ability to look after my daughter, I was often asked, " How will you deal with a young girl going through puberty?"
(If I knew what puberty was I could have answered them).
For her sake I had to try to understand women and their problems a bit better.
So, determined that I would be both mother and father to my Sam, I took up dressmaking and together we would work out how to make shorts, skirts and other items of clothing.

It saved me a fortune, especially as I had to give up adult cabaret and learn to be a Children's Entertainer. That way I could do shows in the daytime and at weekends, and was able to take Sam with me. I needed a whole new wardrobe of show business clothing, so with my new skills I was able to make them for myself, and save money.

I found that the women in the drapery shop, both staff and public wanted to help me. I got advice on cut, style, over locking, collars and patterns as well as praise for my efforts. I was the centre of attraction whenever I went into the shop and if I asked a question like " Why don't my collars come out equal?" The ladies would carefully explain and show me what I was doing wrong. I'd expected them to laugh at me and say. " Well You're a Man ". But once they knew I was serious and having a go, they couldn't help enough.

I made an effort to talk to Sam about anything, and I knew that one day the dreaded PMT would rear it's head. I'd experienced it to a great extent (*Not knowing what it was*), whilst living with my wife and two stepdaughters for twelve years.

" Why is one of you always in a shitty mood?" I'd shout, being answered with a grunt and a stare that would halt a charging bull.

By the time Sam was about ten or eleven, sanitary towels were being advertised on TV for the first time, and whenever the advert for " Wings " came on the box, I'd say "What do they do Sam? Do y'a think they make you fly?" She'd raise her eyebrows and answer " Don't be stupid Dad". (A *phrase she often uses to this day*).

At the age of eleven she began having stomach aches. I was sure this was it, and started thinking about how I would explain periods. *(A subject I can never fully understand as a male of the species)*.

One Thursday she came home complaining about her stomach. I knew it was time to face my nemesis, and as I stood at the sink doing the washing up, I started to edge towards the subject." Sam. You know these stomach aches you've been having? There's something that happens to women. I don't really know how it feels, but I know it's a bit messy, and it happens every month for a few days and…" She put her hands on her hips and said " Dad. I'm not having a period. I just have stomach ache. OK ". With that one sentence my long-suffering fear of this subject was banished.

Over the next few years I asked many questions of the women around me, so that I could help Sam with the problem of this womanly curse.

We'd purchase herbal remedies like Evening Primrose together, to try and ease her PMT, and sometimes I'd call up the isle of the supermarket. " Sam. Do you want strap on or Tuck in Sanitary Towels?" *(Much to her embarrassment)*. I remember one conversation with my sister about training bras. She'd offered to take Sam to buy one, I asked " Why does she need a bra when she hasn't got anything to put in it?" The logic of my man's mind never really understood her answer, which went something like." If she thinks she needs a bra, she'll feel grown up". I decided then that, there are some things I don't need to understand.

If the end result is harmony- I just do as I am advised *(Note I don't say told.)*

After years of questioning and experimentation: To all men I give my answer to softening the heart of a menstruating woman. CHOCOLATE. It works on almost all female ailments; headaches, bad moods, and PMT will all be eased with this sweet brown substance. It may not cure the symptoms completely but with most women, a hug and a bar of chocolate will bring a smile and soften her heart towards you. Of course you have to experiment. I for instance have found women who want, Licorice, Baileys, and even Pickled Onions at certain times of the month. But with a little time and effort you can find the magic ingredient, and then harmony can be achieved almost every day.

Now back to the poem. Of course my dream was simply that. I never won the pools or any other competition.

Except the morning Sam woke me up by stuffing a brown envelope up my nose. On opening the letter I saw a cheque from the premium bonds. It was a strange one, instead of the sum being written in words, it had boxes, which were crossed denoting, Tens, Hundreds, and Thousands of pounds. I looked carefully and saw that I'd won fifty thousand pounds. "What?".

I jumped out of bed and rubbed my eyes. The box marked thousands had a cross in it. "Yippee". I ran into the toilet and as I sat with the cheque in my mouth, I rubbed my eyes with a wet flannel. Taking the now damp money order out of my mouth, I looked again. Fifty Thousand Pounds.

" I can pay off all my debts and still have enough for a Harley "I thought. Returning to the bedroom I put down the cheque but continued to look at it, as I got dressed (*in case it was a dream*).

Once dressed, I picked up the money order and went into the kitchen, where I turned on the kettle and sat at the table looking at the box marked " Fifty Thousand Pounds". My eyes never left the cheque until the kettle boiled and after making my coffee I returned to look at it. But now the cross had changed boxes. FIFTY POUNDS. "Look harder" I thought. FIFTY POUNDS. Running back into the bathroom I rubbed my eyes once more with the wet flannel. May be the cross will move back. FIFTY POUNDS it said. Keep looking. No I had only won fifty quid. (*The rest of the day was a bit of an anti climax*).

I still have my hundred Premium Bonds, but in the twenty or so years since. I've won, nothing else, zilch, nada, fuck all.

I never found my maiden again but sometimes when I get a pile of letters I have a little twinge of hope that one of them might just be a cheque from the Premium Bonds.

Ode To The Brussel Sprout

It's Green and bulbous with white veins
Just like those of Varicose
It smells when boiled or steamed
Just like sewage overflows

It's eaten in quantities so vast
It causes methane to be passed
So why do mothers make us eat
This gastronomic anti-treat ?

Whilst visiting my house one day my mother stood talking to my elderly neighbour. The neighbour placed a cup of tea and a bag of tomatoes for me on the wall between us. My mother drank the tea and took up the tomatoes saying, " He doesn't drink tea and he hates tomatoes". She was referring to my habits of twenty-five years before.
(*In a mothers eyes we will always be children*).

One evening when I was 35 years old I was having dinner with my mother. I noticed a lone brussel sprout on my plate. (*My dislike for this vegetable is one of the few things that have not changed with adult hood*). I ate around it until she became aware of what I was doing and said *(as she had a thousand times before)* " *I only gave you one sprout so eat it- it's good for you*". I wrote this ode for all children who are faced with consuming this vile tasting abomination. But more than that I realise my mother's perceived nagging is in fact love and consideration. She only wants me to be healthy. However knowing that will never make brussels taste nice to me.
So now a vegetable story.

I have a friend called Daff. We met over thirty years ago, when I fed her dog a packet of cheeslets in a pub. The dog is relevant because I'm allergic to them, and as far as I am concerned the only good dog is the one under the wheels of my jeep. *(Now I've upset a few people, sorry man mode again.*).
This makes our chance meeting even stranger than it was. Subsequently over the years we have remained close friends through two marriages, affairs, births, deaths, and mothers.

17

We've spent many holidays together and shared our innermost feelings.

I once asked Daff how I would know if a woman liked me. She said, " When a woman likes you, her nipples go hard". (*What a load of crap*). Every time I walked on a cold beach, or by a chilly swimming pool, I thought all the women fancied me. I got loads of slaps before I found Daff's advice was Duff!

I know my poem is about brussel sprouts but I have to tell you about another vegetable, which is so abhorrent to me that the taste upon my pallet makes me instantly retch – followed quickly by loud and extreme vomiting. That vegetable is the parsnip.

I met Daff a few years before I was married and in keeping with her duff advice she convinced me that marriage was great. I got married and some months later, she got divorced. In our many and varied conversations the subject of Parsnips never came up. Until.

One Christmas day she invited my self and my new family to dinner. On arriving we were told that her new partner had gone to the allotment on his bike to get fresh vegetables for dinner. The allotment was about thirty minutes' ride away, and we were suitably wined and entertained until he came back.

As the nine of us sat around the kitchen table, Daff started to bring out the dinners. Mine seemed to be buried under a pile of roasted parsnips.

My heart froze. Suddenly I felt sick from the pit of my stomach.

How could I tell Daff of my utter hatred of the parsnip, when her partner had gone to such trouble on Christmas day?

I couldn't. So I tried to mash them up a bit, but their volume only grew. I offered some to my wife, who just shook her head and smiled. Then when Daff wasn't looking I placed one on each of the kid's plates. They just put them back on mine. Finally I had no option. Using a magician's palm, I placed them one by one into my trouser pocket.

Seeing my plate empty of vegetables, Daff disappeared into the kitchen, returning with a bowl of parsnips, several of which she put onto my plate as she said, " These home grown parsnips are lovely aren't they?" I managed to squeeze one more into my pocket, before using the excuse that I was full up and couldn't eat another thing.

This of course meant that I couldn't have any Christmas pudding, Cheese and biscuits, or after eight mints (*all of which I love*). I spent the next few hours with the now puréed parsnips oozing through my trousers and pants.

Many years later I told Daff, and she just laughed. I know now that she wouldn't have been offended. No one would. It was just the man in me making the wrong decision.

So " Why do men lie "? In some cases I think it's because they don't want to hurt someone.

Often when I was a young man, I'd meet a male friend and stop chatting with them for ages.

Rather than tell my wife the truth and risk accusations of being with another woman, or that I'd rather be with my mate than her. I'd say " I got a puncture" or "The car broke down ". Obviously these lies didn't stand up to scrutiny, and we'd end up in a row and not talking for hours.

I once had a friend, whose wife always knew when he lied, (*probably because he was such a bad liar*). She'd just give him a look which told him she knew, and he'd spend days feeling guilty. I don't know if it ever stopped him lying, but she knew her vengeance was in his own feelings of guilt, which he pacified by buying her very expensive presents. (*Don't get mad. Get a present.*)

Ode to the Brussel Sprout was in a small way a dig at my mother. Even today at the age of ninety-one, she will place one sprout on my plate in the hope that I might eat it. It is hidden under the potatoes or a pile of peas.For some reason known only to her, she boils all meat, fries eggs in water, and produces roast potatoes by par boiling, and then frying them in a saucepan of cooking oil. After every meal cooked for me she'll ask, " Was it alright?" To which I answer " Lovely ". So are all lies told by men bad?

I love my mother and have lived with her for the last eight years since my father died. When Sam was young she was always there for us. If I needed advice on illness, or girl's moods, my mother always answered my questions with wise council. She criticises my ironing and in her eyes my cooking is slap- dash.

But when I was offered a part in a TV programme, or a late night cabaret spot, she would baby sit without any prior notice at all. The house I live in with my mother now has to be quiet by ten at night. No cooking after seven and I live with my nemesis " The cat from hell". When my mother asks " Am I stopping you from getting on with you're life? " I say, " No Mum, of course you're not ".

For my mother I eat just one brussel sprout. I swallow half a parsnip, and I lie to her every day. So one has to ask the question " Are all lies bad?"

I mentioned my eccentric friends in the introduction and Daff has to be one. You're going to hear more stories about her as we go along. But when it comes to food she is an Oxymoron.
For over twenty years she's been a Vegetarian.
Except when she comes to my house for dinner.
When my mother (*who is now 91 years old*) cooks her Lamb.
I don't know how it started but the best-kept secret in Daffs life is that she eats lamb. Well there was another time when she went out for Christmas dinner with her own mum. Having been to the ladies room she returned to her mother who told her " I've ordered for you. I know you're a vegetarian so I've ordered you chicken".

As we're on the subject of food I suppose I'd better tell you the story about my Mum's eggs.
In the 80s Edwina Curry, the then food minister caused a minor uproar when she brought to notice a high rate of salmonella poisoning caused by eggs.

For some reason, known only to my Mum, she decided that if you cooked the egg for twice as long as recommended, you wouldn't get the bug. Thereafter eggs were fried for 5 minutes. Boiled for 20. Poached for 10 and scrambled for 15. I don't think I need to describe the outcome. This didn't really affect me until Sam and I came to live with her.

My Father had recently died and each morning she would cook me egg and bacon just as she had for my Dad. Repeated refusal of breakfast fell on deaf ears and eventually for the sake of peace, I would eat the rubber like fried egg and pale bacon each morning. Long after the health scare had vanished eggs were still cooked in this fashion and everyone who knew us made a point of telling my Mum " Sorry I don't like eggs". Any one who comes to our house is offered food and drink and many times friends have outwitted me and said to my mother " Don't forget I don't like eggs" and then tucked into sausage and mash, smiling as my face contorted at consuming a solidified egg.

Once I was in Sainsbury's shopping with a friend, when she asked if I needed any eggs. In graphic detail I stood and told her how I couldn't face eggs because of the way my Mum cooked them. The next week I was in the café after shopping when a complete stranger said to her friend. " That's Him ". They must have seen my bewildered face, because they came over and said " I heard you telling that lady about your Mum's eggs last week. My mum used to do the same thing". We all had a coffee and I made a new friend.

For many years I consumed those eggs with grace and even on the one occasion when I had to go and throw up, I thanked my mum for the breakfast. Why? Well as we go on you will hear about my youth and the nights I'd stay out till the early hours of the morning. When I came home my dinner was always on a plate balanced over a pan of hot water. My mum's bedroom light was never turned off until I came in and even though my morning coffee sometimes had a tea bag in the bottom, it was always by my bed at 8 am.

I told the egg story at my fortieth birthday to two hundred guests. Daff who was sat next to my mother told me that she was shocked at the revelation and from that day on my eggs come almost uncooked. My boiled eggs come with raw yolks and my fried eggs look like something that's been sneezed up. I still eat them with grace and say thanks. But sometimes I make a point of leaving before my Mum gets up.

It seems a little unfair to pick only on the sprout and the parsnip because there are some meats that defy culinary understanding. For instance why would anyone want to eat pig's liver, kidney, or tripe? Snake, octopus, and squid all taste ok if you don't know what you're eating. But you can't hide the taste of offal! Perhaps I'll write a poem about that one day.

But I do have a sort of offal story.
One day when I was about twelve years old. My nephew Gary and I had been mucking about in the garden. My dad had a small shed and we'd been trying to get diesel to explode by putting some between two metal plates and hitting them as hard as we could with a big hammer. We must have been bright to know that diesel explodes under pressure.

But it didn't make a big enough bang. So being around Nov 5th we went and brought some fireworks. After dismantling a banshee and re building it with added gun powder from some bangers we re assembled it in a toilet roll holder and marvelled as it blew up sending lumps of molten chemicals past our ears.

Next we got a metal tube and sealed one end. Loading it with gunpowder and wadding made from rag we dropped in a ball bearing before finally throwing in the lighted touch paper from a banger. The whole thing blew apart in Gary's hands. So he went into the bathroom to wash them

Meanwhile my dad had arrived home with a freshly killed Chicken. This wasn't uncommon, as my dad would often stop the steam train he was driving to pick mushrooms or kill a rabbit to bring home. Strangely enough even with these un scheduled stops the trains ran on time.

Mum plucked the bird and held it over the outside drain as she cut off the head.

With her hand pushed deep into the body of the animal, she heard a gurgle and proceeded to launch the Chicken up the garden screaming.

Gary and I rushed out from the bathroom just in time to see my Mum realise that the gurgling was the water Gary had let out of the sink, which was running down the drain. The bird was recovered and we ate it for dinner along with one brussel sprout. Well actually dinner was more fun when Gary was there because he eats anything, so I would just give him the veg from my plate when my Mum wasn't looking.

Why?

Somewhere a baby cries, through fear
hunger or pain.
An old man sits in a small cold room.
Alone again
A teenager dies from an overdose of
drugs.
Which he thought were cool
A woman screams at her partner.
In another nightly brawl.

A bomb explodes ripping through rooms.
Hurling bodies through windows.
Casting devastation and doom.
Somewhere a door is opened,
Splintering from its frame.
Someone's prized possessions are being
obtained.

Those which have no monetary value.
Will be discarded and thrown away.
Insurance policies left.
So the owner can be robbed again
another day.

As these things happen we strive to conquer space.
To spread the seed of the human race.
More likely to leave a world in ruin.
Pollution and hatred all our own doing.

But before we leave this world behind.
Should we not take the time to find.
A little humanity from man to mankind?

For several years in the late 80's I worked as a walk-on in television. I made a good living being one of the regular extras in programmes like Eastenders and The Bill. When working on these jobs *(which may last only one day),* you learn to make friends quickly. Certainly the saying " A stranger is just a friend you haven't met" would be the case here

One day I found myself talking to a young woman who had the night before been burgled for the third time in a year. At one point she was arranging by telephone for the locks to be changed on her flat. There was little emotion in her voice and she later told me that she had no sentimental items left in her possession, and cared little for the goods lost.

The thieves had left her insurance documents in a pile on the coffee table. *(One can only surmise so that the money for the goods lost could be collected, and more purchased for a future burglary).*

I watched the news that night and realised that I accepted tragedy and death with little emotion. I watched as Bob Geldoff appealed for money, using pictures of starving and sick African children to validify his cause. That night the news became more than an inconvenience between films. World news came closer to where I stood and my world became larger than just my family.

As I wrote the poem *why* I vowed to always try to empathise with the misfortune of others. I can't say that I have achieved anything like unilateral empathy but the consideration of others misfortune helps me to realise the good fortunes of my own life, and prompts me to share them with others.

I remember reading somewhere the statement: *" **If the death of a stranger hurt each of us as much as that of a friend or relative there would be no killing** "*. Or maybe I made it up.

This poem has more to do with my emotions as a man than with the subject matter. I was brought up in the days when boys were programmed to feel responsible and be men. Providing money and a home for their family. To show worry or fear is to admit failure as a man.I was lucky. I had a mum and a dad; they stayed together until death parted them. Their guidance was good and firm and I only once saw my father shed a tear, and then only for a brief moment when I shared with him my feelings of desperation, during divorce. Just one single tear rolled from each of our eyes and then it was never spoken of again. I don't think we exchanged the words " I love you " but I'm sure we both knew that we did. We never hugged, and I never showed weakness in front of him. I'm sure that I'm not the only man to have been instilled with the feeling that to share a problem is a weakness and to show empathy will emasculate us.

I've learned many things since that time, and now talk freely about my feelings. Women often ask me " Why won't men talk about their problems?". The answer I think is simple. They're afraid to. My fear of perceived failure has cost me relationships and caused many hours of sulking alone. Even now I can't say how to get a man to share his problems. Patience could be one answer.

If I knew in my early years what I know now, so many of the things I saw as problems could have been solved by a simple hug – but I probably wouldn't have accepted it.

Enough of the philosophical stuff – time for another story.

The jobs on offer as an extra varied from calls with only one or two people and epics with hundreds of extras. In one episode of Casualty, there was a disaster in a football ground. The production could only afford a few hundred extras, so we spent four days standing in the rain, being moved around the stadium as the camera shots changed, so it looked like there was a big crowd. For the most part, contrary to general belief, this job has little or no glamour. Let me tell you about " Four Minute Mile ".
As you would expect it was about the first man to run the four-minute mile. The time period in which it was set was as far as I can remember the nineteen thirties. In their wisdom, makeup had decided that all the men would have a short back and sides hair cut.
So at 6-30 am four hundred extras lined up like something from the great holocausts moving slowly towards a porta-cabin . Inside we sat six in a row whilst a pair of electric clippers shaved the back and sides of our heads.
Once cropped we exited from a door at the far end of the cabin, and at the bottom of the steps a girl from costume, handed each of us a balaclava.

WHY?

Why did they shave our heads and then give us a hat?
Many of the extras were, however happy to have the
haircut, as we were paid £8 extra for it.

I should explain that in those days almost all the
Cabaret and Variety acts I knew, made up their
money by working as extras or walk-ons.

During the filming of this production, lots of the
people I knew in the entertainment world got a few
days work on it.

So for the next six or eight weeks, every live show I
appeared in saw the Comedians, Musos, Comperes,
Jugglers, Children's Entertainers and Magicians all
wearing Baseball caps or some other inappropriate
head gear on stage, to hide their "*four minute mile*"
hair cuts.

For me the best thing about film work was the food.
We were fed things I could never have afforded to
buy for myself. During my days in TV I was given
everything from Frog's legs to caviar. But one day
whilst working on " The Bill" we were offered a cold
selection of seafood for starters. As the cast and crew
always got to eat first, those of us at the lower end of
the pecking order would pig out on the cold selection
before queuing for the hot dinner.

The problem this day did not become apparent until
about 36 hours later, when every one I knew on the
set went down with the runs. A short while after
during a live show I was working in, every act at
some point used the bucket in my dressing room.

The Comedian had to leave the stage with a radio mike and tell jokes whilst sitting on the toilet.

The audience laughed more heartily at what they thought were toilet humour sound effects and our laughter was even greater knowing that they weren't sound effects.
In fact I think all of our washing machines worked overtime that week.

The Black River

A halo of red appears at the edge of the
night sky.
Heralding the arrival of the morning
sun.
It climbs slowly above the swaying trees.
Waking the birds as it warms the frosted
breeze.

A kestrel hovers whilst the dawn chorus
sings.
Motionless it waits on silent wing.
He dips and rises on the wind.
To see what breakfast daytime brings.

Rabbits pop from banks and hedges.
Fox and Badger hurry to secret places.
The day is new and nature reigns.
With wildlife playing chasing games

The sun shines down on the river of
black.
Smooth and shimmering plain and flat.
It runs on to the horizon with no clear
end.
Then trickles past on its way back again.

In the distance some unknown thing.
Moves towards this tranquil scene.
It's roar becomes louder till heard every
where.
Now the vision approaching is as big as
a bear.

All creatures return to their homes
underground.
As the monster roars past throwing
smoke all around.
It's followed by hundreds and thousands
more.
All dripping oil on the motorway floor.

The Kestrel looks down on this un
natural scene.
At the river of black where once green
fields had been.

I like *The Black River,* am I allowed to say that? Well it's my poem so I'm going to.

At the age of forty I went back to school, just to see if I could have passed any academic exams.

The man in me refused to take a GCSE and I joined up for A level English and Literature. I decided to take both in the same year at night school.

After my first essay (*which was only two thousand words*), came back with over a hundred spelling and grammatical mistakes I had to own up to the tutor that I'd left school at fourteen and didn't know a noun from an adjective (*Still don't*).

He was brilliant and it turned out that the rest of the class didn't know either. So we were given extra tutoring in language. He was the man that introduced me to Men are from Mars Women are from Venus and the whole class came to my house so that he could help us to understand Shakespeare. *(That was a bit embarrassing for him as our Literature tutor was crap so I paid him £45 a night to teach us privately).*

At the time I was embroiled in the Poems and letters of John Keats. Each week I took one day off and I'd ride out to a National Trust house on my Harley – where I would sit and look to the clouds imagining that the great romantic poets may have sat in that very place. I didn't write any great poetry whilst I was there. Actually I have never written any great poetry. But in the early morning when I rode along the A27, just west of Emswoth. I'd see a kestrel hovering beside the motorway.

He seemed to be in the same place each time I passed. So in my heightened state of awareness for nature and her creatures, I imagined the changes seen by the animals and birds that made their homes near by.

Then I began to think about the dramatic changes mankind had made to the landscape in only a few years, and in humbleness to that bird I wrote *The Black River*. By the way I passed the A level and got a C.
The link to my next story is that it contains animals and water.

When I was twenty-one, I got married and inherited a family of three children.
One Sunday morning, I walked round to the local newsagents to get a paper, leaving my wife and children having breakfast. On the way I ran into my friend Roger, who was making big money in the car business.
He told me he was on his way to go fishing in his new boat and asked if I'd like to go with him. I just forgot that I was married and jumped into his car. I know what you're thinking but it's true. I just forgot, OK!
An hour later we were chugging out of Chichester Harbour in his new Micro-Plus Day Cruiser, when I remembered my new family. "Shit I didn't tell Lyn where I was going". With no mobile phone I couldn't do anything about it so we anchored and began assembling our fishing gear.
At the time we both considered ourselves to be macho men. We raced Hot- Rods, drank Spirits by the bottle, and faced down any threat with a look that would freeze the hearts of all but the most psychopathic men.

However when we opened the newspaper wrapping and looked at the wriggling rag worms brought for bait, we stopped in our tracks.

"Fancy a lager? " Roger asked, as he walked away from the worms". Before I could answer he added, " You bait up the hooks, I'll get the beer".

I knew rag worms had pincers and could bite, so I waited until his return. As I took the can of beer from him we both sat down and looked at the pale slimy hermaphrodites, which were wriggling out of their newspaper wrapping and onto the seat beside us. Edging away like frightened rabbits (*but of course showing no fear*), Roger poked me in the arm and said " Put them back in the paper ". " Bollocks you put them back " I replied. Roger stood up (*which allowed me to move a little further away from the advancing army of pincer snapping wrigglers*), and went into the galley, returning a minute later wearing a pair of bright yellow marigold rubber gloves. Confidently he scraped together the worms and after installing two onto our fishing hooks, put the rest back in the newspaper wrapping. " Just put the gloves on so that I could grip them better " he said.

After looking around to make sure that no passing mariners had seen his gloves, he quickly removed the embarrassing items and threw them on the floor of the boat. We popped open another can of lager and lowered our fishing lines into the water.

For about an hour we sat drinking lager and talking about cars and motorbikes, money and women, then. Roger reached out and grabbed his rod just as it was about to be dragged over the side of the boat. With the rod bending in an arc, he started to reel in his line.

Looking to the place where it entered the water we began to see something silver spinning just under the surface.

Roger shouted to me " You grab it when it gets to the side of the boat ". By now we could clearly see the eel that had taken his bait. It was about three feet long and two inches thick, but seemed like ten feet long and a foot thick, as it spun around tangling itself in the line. " Grab the fucking thing, " he shouted. "Bollocks " was my reply. By now the eel has managed to wrap itself around the end of Rogers's fishing rod and was only a few feet away from us.

I remembered a fishing story I'd read once about a boat that was found somewhere with a twelve foot moray eel in the bottom, and when they cut it open the fisherman was inside.

Suddenly Rogers rod came flying past me, eel still wrapped around it. It splashed into the sea sinking beneath the waves.

We packed up the remaining rod and threw the worms overboard in silence; bobbing around in the middle of the harbour we finished our beers and cleaned up. Then we pulled up the anchor and headed back to the mooring. The boat was tied up and the gear that was left put in the boot of the car. Nothing was said about the eel or the worms. We knew our secret was safe. (*Until now*).

About five thirty that evening I walked up my garden path trying to think of a good story. Of course my wife was more than just a little angry, and on hearing the expected question " Where the fuck have you been?" I gave my half rehearsed reply.

" I had to go on a breakdown ".

By the time I'd answered the next five questions starting with "How can you go on a breakdown with no tools?" I'd dug a hole for myself that was so big; there was no hope of escape.

The row that followed included accusations of my being with another woman and ended with my wife crying and saying that she thought I had been run over and was worried sick.

I never told her the truth. Why? Because I would have had to tell her that I forgot I was married or even worse admit my fear of worms.

That boat got wrecked in the gales of '87. It ended up in the lounge bar of the Crab and Lobster pub. I think in all I was involved in four boats with my old mate Roger. One was a seven-ton Gin palace, which broke down every time we went out in it. I remember once the rudder fell off because we were not sure if you go to the right or left of the green buoys and hit a sand bank. Roger was pissed as usual and insisted on phoning the AA on his mobile. Believe it or not once the woman on the phone realised we were in a boat, she got the Harbour Master to come and help us. That boat got woodworm or the maritime version of it, and Roger sold it to some guy who grounded it on a mud flat and lived there for years. The next boat we owned together never actually made it into the water.

Just for fun we would go to ministry auctions and buy job lots. We brought everything from fibreglass matting to axel grease. Then we would make it a quest to sell it on for a profit. Roger kept the kitty and one day called me to say we had bought a boat.

This boat about 30 feet long and ten feet high, out of the water, its greatest value being that it had a toilet.

A great piece of machinery which allowed you to (*after using it*), pump up and down a lever which would munch up the contents and throw them out the side of the boat. "A real man's toy".

The boat itself was not quite sea worthy, so we had it delivered by low loader to Rogers's barn at a cost of £125, where we wedged it precariously upright. After smashing off the cabin because it made the boat to high to get through the barn doors.

We had every intension of renovating that boat, and at least three times over the next two years we opened the doors and pumped the handle on the toilet.

I got a phone call one day to tell me that Roger had found a bloke who wanted to buy it, and I just knew my old mate would have made a profit on the sale.

By the time we came to the last boat, both Roger and I had become able to laugh at our watery misfortunes. We didn't tell many other people of our stupidity, but in a male bonding type of way we did laugh together.

Whilst at yet another ministry auction Roger obtained a dinghy. Not any old dingy but one like the SAS use for covert missions. Complete with trailer and 40 horse Johnson outboard.

A second hand Land Rover was purchased to pull it with and the boat was loaded with, fishing rods, life jackets, bait, and a cool box containing sandwiches and lager. We decided to launch the dinghy from Selsey beach.

We chose a back street which lead to an opening onto the stones. The beach fell away at an angle of about 45 degrees and dropped about 15 feet onto the sand. Bravely Roger drove straight onto the stones dragging the boat and trailer down onto the sand and into the water.

Once the Land Rover was up to its axels in the surf, we jumped out (*Forgetting we only had trainers on*) straight into the sea.

After the initial shock of wet feet, we began un hooking the trailer. With the Land Rover back on the sand we untied the boat. The water was above the trailer wheels, so the dinghy started to float around and be buffeted against the metal stays of the trailer. I pulled it away from under the boat leaving Roger clinging to the side. As I placed the trailer down on the beach I heard Roger shout " O Shit ". A large wave had lifted the dinghy and smashed it against the breakwater, the force of an outgoing wave dragged it along, and a bolt ripped into the side. Within seconds the boat started to fill with water, and before I could get the trailer back under it. It sank.

We gathered up the rods and cool box, which were now drifting away with the tide, and managed to get the boat half on the trailer. Then we noticed the tide was coming in, (*bad time to try and launch a boat*) and we had no chance of getting the Land Rover hooked up. So we tied the mooring rope from the boat to the tow hook of the rover and I began to inch the trailer towards the shore. Having only achieved a few feet, all four wheels of the vehicle began to spin, sinking into the wet sand up to the axels. Now the water was lapping around the bottom of the driver's door. With the rope untied I gunned the engine changing from first to reverse in an effort to elongate the sand ruts and drive out. Eventually with the clutch smelling of burning asbestos I pulled the Land Rover up onto the stones.

After about an hour of tugging the half loaded boat up the beach inch by inch and then waiting for the clutch to cool down whilst water ran out of the boat, we arrived back on the road, tied what was left of the dinghy onto the trailer and hooked the whole lot back onto the land rover.

Soaking wet and absolutely knackered we sat in the gutter, me with a coke and Roger with a lager. Suddenly Roger stood up, picking up the cool box and the rods, he said " Come on, there's a jetty round the corner. We can fish off of there."

As we rounded the raised narrow path towards a concrete jetty, which ran about 100 yards into the sea, a round of applause from a group of bird watchers greeted us. " We've been watching you two nutters. You're completely mad, and he's got it all on tape". One of the group held up a video camera. We smiled with embarrassment and made our way to the end of the jetty where Roger consumed the rest of the lager and after a respectable time we left.

Believe it or not, a new clutch was fitted to the Land Rover. The dinghy was mended with the aid of the biggest puncture repair kit in the world, and the whole lot once again, sold for a profit (*If I know my old mate Roger*).

By this time in my life, I was able to laugh at the stupid things I do when I go into "Man Mode". I can still see Roger's wife rolling her eyes and saying " Its exactly what I would expect of you two ".

I know now that if we had had a woman with us when the boat sank, she would have taken the time to think about the situation; Gathered up the floating equipment and put it in the Land Rover. Tied the boat to the breakwater and gone to the pub for lunch, whilst waiting for the tide to go out.

The water would have drained from the dinghy. The sand would be dry, and we wouldn't have looked like prats. Come to think of it, if we had had a woman with us, the boat probably wouldn't have got damaged. No to tell the truth we would have just ignored her and done the same thing?

Vocation

I could have been a doctor, an artist or a
cook.
I may have won a nobel prize.
Or written an important book.
But at the time it seemed more fun,
to simply play around
So at the age of thirty-four.
I've no vocation found.

It may be wrong to think this way.
But if I had to give life up.
I'd like to have a new one.
As a kitten or a pup.

To sleep all day and wake for food.
Have casual sex when in the mood.
Whoever said man was supreme.
Has obviously never seen.
A household pet, pampered all it's life.
No stress, No strain, No nagging wife.

So if I get a second chance.
Don't send me back to sing and dance.
A little cat will be just fine.
Or anything but not mankind

At the time I thought I had written a poem about our cats. Yes I know I am allergic to cats and dogs. But I thought my daughter was lonely, and with her sisters gone and the stress of the divorce I thought a cat might be good for her.

Tiggy – that's what we called him, (*I was still going through that phase when I didn't want another "She " in my house*). He was a small tabby cat, who lived happily with us for about a year. One day my neighbour, Mrs C said" Your cat's pregnant ".

I quickly replied, " It can't be it's a boy". "Fraid not " she said. Then she gave me a biology lesson about felines.

A few weeks later, in the bottom draw of an upstairs room, I found five kittens. One of which was dead. Sam was at school, so I sat for a while trying to decide what to do with the dead Kitten. My brain said " chuck it in the bin " but my heart told me to bury it in the garden. I'd grown to like Tiggy and it seemed horrible to just throw one of her babies away, so I buried it under the front hedge, which had become our animal graveyard.

When Sam was asleep Tiggy would often sit on my chest with her head by my ear purring softly, until my sneezing jerked her away. I guess this little cat was in some way a companion for me, that is, until an elderly neighbour with Alzheimer's enticed her away with food (*Typical female, got a better offer and went off, sorry that's man -mode*).

The poem *Vocation* is I suppose about the cat and me. By this time in my life I had been: a Motor Mechanic, Coal Man, Lorry driver, Fairground owner, DJ, Cabaret artist, and MOT inspector. Several of which I worked in at the same time.

The aim of my poem is to express my feelings that it must be more fun to be a cat than a man. Tiggy obviously was getting more sex than me, and two lots of food. *Bitch.*

Alongside this was my own insecurity about my various careers, which seemed to others exiting and interesting occupations, but offered me little prospects for long-term success. I considered getting a regular job, but came to the conclusion that it was too hard. Working from home suited my situation, so I continued to work in a variety of occupations, which allowed me flexibility with my working hours.

Tiggy had a son called Junior who grew to be as big as a dog. Junior left home with his mum and both lived happily with the old lady whose Alzheimer's meant she met them for the first time, every day. When they were ill or misbehaved she would miraculously remember that they were "My Cats", and the rest of the time, deny all knowledge of them. When she died they were unceremoniously delivered to me in a basket for disposal, by her family whose only concern was that the cats wouldn't pester the people they'd sold the house to. Sam took their leaving us in her stride, but another cat came into our lives a little later on.

My father died when Sam was about fourteen. Being close to her Grandparents, she left me in my house opposite and went to live with my mother.

After about a year and continual nagging from both Sam and my mother. I moved in with them, my mum, who was then in her eighties decided that Sam wanted a cat. So off to the RSPCA rescue centre she went, and came back with " The Cat From Hell".

This thing is like no cat I'd ever met. Its meow is as loud as a car stereo; its fur is like brown wire, and falls out in clumps. It dribbles, shits everywhere, and hates me.

My bedroom is upstairs, and next to my door is a panel leading to the loft. The cat sits outside my door all night, banging up against the hatch at irregular intervals, keeping me awake. Then when I open my bedroom door in order to launch it down the stairs on the end of my boot (*which I have put on especially for the job*) it runs between my legs and we have a half hour game of hide and seek around my bedroom, with the cat occasionally stopping to shit in the corner.

My mother knows I hate the cat and often says, " I can't go until the cat is dead. He wont look after it and no one else would want it"(*I have to wonder. How long do cats live?*)

I've tried: Sodium Chloride in its water, a blanket under the rear wheels of my Jeep,

letting a dog into the garden, and accidentally locking it in the shed for three days. It won't die. Every one thinks I'm paranoid. But after a few days of knowing Misty they all have to agree, she is " The Cat From Hell ".

The story I'm going to tell you now contains nearly as much disappointment for me as my earlier premium bonds win. It happened one morning in early spring.

After getting dressed I quietly crept down the stairs. It's a game I play with my mother. Every morning as I get to the bottom step, she leaps out of the kitchen door and asks,

" What do you want for breakfast?"- "Nothing thanks mum". - " You must have something"- " No thanks" – " Fried Egg?"- " No thanks"- " Bacon Sandwich?" " No Thanks"- " Sausages?"- " No thanks"- " I'll make you some toast then ".

This morning she wasn't there. Shit where is she? - She's died in her sleep. - Fuck. I wish I'd given her more time. - Damn I've got a show this afternoon. - I'll have to wait for the funeral directors, - wonder if they will come quickly? - Will I get to the gig on time?

Better go and look in her bedroom.

Looking around her bedroom door, which is always ajar, I'm afraid of what waits inside. I see a neatly made bed on which is placed my mum's coat and her handbag. " She must have died in the garden. (Damn). I'm going to have to carry my mum's body into the house.

As I head towards the back door, I see her from the corner of my eye. She's sitting in her chair, speaking into the telephone. " He'll be glad. Well it's best she went before me- OK I'll see you later". Putting down the phone she noticed me standing by the door and in a soft sad voice said. " Misty has been run over". Holding a non-committal face and a formal stance my whole being cried, " YES-YES- The Fucking Cat is Dead – I do believe in God – I will pay my taxes- Let's have a party".

My mum continued, " She must have got run over early this morning – I've wrapped her in that old piece of cloth you left in the conservatory. Will you bury her? "Course I will mum ".

As I looked at the package lying by the back door, I didn't care that my mother had wrapped the dead cat in the red velvet drape, which had been part of my Children's show for the last ten years. No didn't care at all " The Cat Is Dead".

A little smile of satisfaction grew on my face, with every thrust of the spade. I was so happy digging that hole. I made it much bigger and deeper than necessary. Then I took one last look at my Nemesis before dispatching it to the bowels of the earth from whence it came. Yep that was Misty all right. A bit flat- but I would know that wiry brown hair anywhere.

As I patted the last spadefull of dirt into place, I took a moment to stand in peace looking at the garden, which seemed to have taken on an air of tranquillity. I noticed birds sitting unharassed on branches. No cat shit on the lawn. I thought," Life is good".

What's that? I felt something brushing up against the inside of my right ankle. Looking down my heart froze. I got that sick feeling you get in your stomach when you've accidentally cut off a finger. There was the cat, alive and mocking me by rubbing against my ankle

I had to dig up the one I had buried, to see if I'd been dreaming, and there it was, crushed but identical.

As I compared the two animals, my mother came out of the house and seeing the cat cried out " Misty ", the cat ran over and jumped into her outstretched arms. Then the two of them disappeared inside, leaving me with the dilemma of burial or dustbin.

Later that day my mother informed me that the dead cat was in fact a new kitten brought for the children of a woman who lived opposite. They didn't have a garden and my mother had offered to bury the dead kitten in our garden so the children could come over after school and place a cross on its place of rest. Looking at my watch I saw that I only had about an hour before the schools came out.

Where were all the bin bags? Shit the dustman's been. Into Man-Mode I go. I decide I'll go to the vets in West Meads and see if I can buy a corpse. But decided that was a stupid idea.

I know, I've got an old brown puppet dog in the garage; I'll wrap that up and bury it.

With only twenty minutes to go I had a brain wave. Hang on. They can't see what's buried under the earth. So I made a nice smooth grave like mound and in due course the children came round, placed a cross at one end, thanked me and went home.

Animals I have known

I had some fish once. When we went on holiday I put in one pinch of food for every day that we were going to be away. If they choose to eat all of the food and explode on the first day. It's not my fault.

For several years I couldn't make out why the bottom of my food cupboards were covered in chocolate sprinkles, *(Especially as I had never brought any)*. Until my mother came over one day and went mad shouting " You will have to call in the council to get rid of these mice".

At about nine o'clock some evenings, Sam and I would watch the two lovely brown and white dogs walk from the field at the back of our garden, across our lawn, up the drive and down the road. Sometimes they'd stop to eat the scraps we put out for the birds. Once they stopped and ate the Rabbit. We'd never seen a fox before.

The animal I want to tell you about now probably does have a name, but I don't know what it is. My encounter happened early one morning in mid winter. It was in the early nineties, when gales and heavy rain were becoming part of our regular weather pattern. This had been a particularly bad week, with trees being ripped from their roots, lorries blown onto their sides, and I met a monster from outer space.

My chosen mode of transport at this time was a white Mk2 Transit van. On the sides in two-foot high letters it read " Pip Frederick Children's Magician. Comedy Magic and Games", (*My daughter hated going to school in that vehicle*). The rear of this van was equipped with, a zed-bed, a cardboard box containing a loaf of bread, margarine, Marmite, and a block of cheese. My chosen luxury items were a six inch colour TV and a spare car battery. *(I always carried that after I ran the van battery flat watching the TV, and had to bump start it by rolling down a hill, in the mud, on my own)*
I'd been booked for a walk-on part in an episode of French and Saunders. The meeting point was a hotel somewhere in the middle of Exmoor. With a 7-30 am call time I had to leave home in Bognor Regis at about 3 am.

Two and a half hours later I found myself driving along an undulating country road in the middle of Exmoor. Occasionally through the driving rain I could see a faint light glimmering in the window of some far off farmhouse, but with the wind threatening to blow my van onto its side at every bend, my concentration was firmly fixed on the road ahead, whilst all outside the beams of my headlights was so black that even the moon couldn't penetrate the darkness.

As I hunched over the steering wheel trying to see further ahead than my lights would allow, I saw an un distinguishable mass in the gloom. I slowed down to a crawl until my headlights fully illuminated the thing, which was blocking my path.

Bringing the van to a standstill about twenty meters from the obstacle, the idling of the engine merged with the wind as I sat in silence for what seemed like minutes, but was in fact only a few seconds.

There in front of me stood a monster from some place other than this world. I remember thinking it was just like I had imagined a Minator or one of those other monsters from Greek Mythology.

It stood about six feet tall, with a head larger than proportionate for its body. Standing solid on its four legs, I could see the tail swinging slowly from one side of its body to the other. Its twelve-inch horns sat above huge red eyes, reflecting the light from my headlights, as its head moved slowly up and down like a snake hypnotising its prey.

I will never know why, but I climbed out of the van and walked slowly towards the monster. With a stare fixed firmly upon me it let out a snort, followed by jets of smoke, which almost reached the spot where I was standing.

In a few seconds I was back in the van with the doors locked. As I revved the engine in panic and tried in vain to find reverse gear, the monster turned slowly and lumbered off through the hedge and disappeared into the blackness of the storm filled night. Once again I was alone in this most inhospitable place, looking for a hotel on a road with no name.

Eventually I found it, or in fact it found me.

As I turned a corner I saw a light and there on the left of the road was a large car park surrounded by overhanging trees and a sign, which read simply Hotel. The only building for miles, I knew this had to be the place. It was 6-30 am, still dark, and with the rain dripping at irregular intervals on to my roof of my van. I sat cold, wet and trembling, in the car park. By about 7 am lights were coming on, and I was able to go into the hotel and make myself known to the crew. Two hot cups of tea and a bacon roll later I climbed into a mini bus with several other extras and we began the journey to the film location.

As we travelled through the open rocky planes of Exmoor now in daylight, I saw my monster standing beside the road, Only now it didn't look so big, and the fire from it's nostrils was a smoky breath in the October frost. The driver of the mini bus interrupted my thoughts, " Have you seen these cows, they only breed them here. Look like monsters don't they?"

There was my answer. The monster from outer space was some sort of cow. It's thick shaggy brown fur, and long horns made it look fearful, and larger than it actually was. In the daylight, the eyes that were reflected red in my van lights were just black, and the dragons fire breath, was only the steam of exhalation on a cold morning.

Night time Seduction

In the silent stillness of the night,
A distant voice is heard.
Interruption from a dream,
Take me, Use me, consume me.
Dark and appealing,
It's voluptuous curves tease and invite.
Pleading, Wake up,
Hold me, Taste me.
Dreams disappear.
As a sweet aroma arouses the senses.
Soft and alluring it begs for attention.
Pangs and longings overtake tiredness
and sensibility.
An outstretched hand reaches for
the siren like bar of chocolate.
Ripping away the covering,
before thrusting pure pleasure deep into
a lusting mouth
Then in the warm satisfaction of a
secret feast,
she drifts quietly back to her place of
dreams.
Leaving me to wonder.
How can I compete with her secret
midnight lover?

When I wake up in the night, I fancy a steak sandwich, or a Kebab. But the women I have known seem on the whole, to crave Chocolate or other sweet foods.

At the beginning of one relationship with a woman who will always be dear to my heart, I would often wake up in the night to find her gone. Hearing cupboards in the kitchen being opened and closed I eventually found that she was on a quest to find anything with chocolate in it, going so far as to eat her children's sweets if nothing else could be found. Then she would return to bed and fall into a deep and relaxed sleep. Leaving me to wonder what a bar of chocolate could do that I couldn't.

Being in my forties and with my quest to understand and interact better with the women in my life, I discussed my feelings with her and began to accept that her midnight chocolate adventures didn't mean that I couldn't satisfy her. She just had a craving for chocolate. In a nutshell that is why I wrote Night time Seduction.

My jealousy towards this in-animate substance was finally banished by filling a drawer next to her with chocolate bars of all types, then she could wake anytime and consume whatever she wanted, and by my supplying the midnight feast I felt in some small way part of her enjoyment in consuming it.

Some years later however I was blamed for her increased weight and although that wasn't the only reason, we parted.

Just to show the lateral tangents that my male mind thinks in, the first story, which springs to mind, is how I met my friend Jenny.

I don't know if she has the same passion for chocolate as my lady, but she does however love sweets, and during our first meeting she consumed many, which were destined for the mouths of children but never made it past her table.

It was Christmas and I'd taken a job as Santa Claus. Two large international companies had put in money to run a charity Santa's Grotto in a large shopping mall in Brighton. It had been specially built into an empty shop unit, and was based on Alice in Wonderland (with a dickens style).

A lovely little woman in a dormouse costume met parents and children at the front door. She had a plate of sweets, which was offered to the children on entering. Then they passed into Santa's lounge, where everything was bigger than normal to give the illusion that they had become smaller. Being directed through the fireplace, they would knock on a door before coming out into the white and windy North Pole. Where they met Santa and got a present.

Thousands of presents had been purchased and wrapped, with pink paper for girls and blue for boys. I got to choose which present I gave, so as is expected of the big man in red, I gave better presents to the good kids. The first week we saw about a hundred kids a day. Then after reading the usual seasonal Santa Horror story in the newspaper, I called the local TV station and told them to come and see the real Santa.

They started by interviewing a local boy, *(who looked surprisingly like Harry Potter)*. He done a survey each year of the local Santa's and we were awarded nine out of ten. *(I don't know what we lost a point for?)*

But we got a ten-minute segment that night on the local news and the next day attendances at our grotto rose to about three hundred.

Sitting along side me was Jenny, dressed in an ill fitting, but well appropriate Mad Hatter suit. She was offering to take anyone's picture with Santa and supply two copies for £2-50. Being self-employed, she only earned money if she took photos.

During the slow times we chatted about any and all subjects, from her boyfriend Martin to the photo's she took as a forensic photographer, whilst working for the police. Eight hours a day for three weeks, we exchanged life stories, stopping regularly for me to pull up my beard and greet visiting families and children.

Most of the time it was a great job. Coffee arrived three or four times a day from the office next door. Women and female college students would insist on sitting on Santa's knee, and for the most part Children would fill my heart with their love for this vast jovial character, that I was playing. Some of them I will never forget.

One day a smart young mother and her neatly dressed five-year-old daughter visited us. The little girl's name was Heather. When I'd finished speaking with her about going to bed early on Christmas eve, and helping mum with the washing up. I asked, " What would you like for Christmas Heather". She replied politely " Could I have my Daddy back please?" Mum explained that her father had been killed in the Falklands war.

Her words were emotionless as she held tight to the little girl's hand, but as I looked into her eyes I saw the pain in her heart that was being hidden from her daughter.

For once in my life I didn't know what to say. I bumbled something like " I can't bring your Daddy back, but Father Christmas will always be there for you. Just send me a letter, any time of year". I gave her one of every girls present I had and like the man I was trained to be showed no emotion as the mother and daughter left. It was a busy afternoon and I had no time to dwell on it that day. However now many years later, I find I have thought of that child almost every Christmas since, and shed a quiet tear for someone I never knew.

Jenny and I had loads of laughs over the weeks, but I often wondered how she earned enough to make it worth sitting all day in the grotto. As each visitor received his or her gift, she would ask " would you like a photo with Santa?" Some did, some didn't. But there were others who took away the smile, which almost always beamed from her face.

One week day afternoon at about 4 pm, just as we were thinking of packing up, a family of six wandered through the door. Mother paid £1, took a handful of sweets and shepherded her family past the dormouse and through the lounge. Without knocking on the door to my North Pole grotto, the family burst in as I quickly pulled up my white beard. " You stand that side Stuart, Gemma you come this side, Harry you stand between his legs. " She stopped to take out a baby from her pushchair, and placing it on my knee with a squelch, said, " There you hold the baby. Have you got the camera dad?"

Granddad rummaged around in the pocket of his grey raincoat, whilst the baby wriggled about on my knee.

As it moved the room filled with a smell, which indicated that the child needed a clean nappy.

" Here it is " said Granddad. Holding up a disc camera. (*Do you remember disc cameras? They were a fad for a couple of years. Bad quality pictures.*) As mother took it I said " Better take the baby back now, we don't want to frighten her do we?" " Alfies a boy, " She said, as she held out the camera to Jenny. Who was standing, stunned by the whole thing. With mum and Granddad squashed in the command was given " Take the picture dear. In fact take two just in case." Jenny did as she was told but I noticed her finger accidentally covering half the lens, and if I know her, a Christmas tree was growing out of someone's head. Photo call over Jenny sat with a face like thunder in the corner of the grotto, sending thoughts of Christmas misery and doom to them. I held out the baby for a second time.

" Better take Alfie back now so that I can find some presents. " You'd never believe it, as I held him out the bloody kid started giggling. " O' he likes you. Hold him a bit longer " said mum. I struggled to hold the baby on my knee with one hand, and reach into my sack to find presents for the other children, (*who although scruffy seemed like good kids*). I then felt the wet patch on the leg of my costume grow at an alarming rate. I thought, " Please let some one else knock on the door, and then I can hurry them off". But no knock came.

Babies usually cry when Santa holds them, but this one absolutely refused and just wriggled around giggling, or gurgling, or whatever babies do when they're happy. Even the full squelching nappy didn't upset this kid. Then. Whaaa . "YES" the baby started to cry. " O dear I think he's had enough."

I said as I handed Alfie back and ushered the family towards the exit. As she passed Jenny, the woman threw one of the handful of sweets she had taken from the dormouse onto Jennies table and said " Thanks for taking the photos."

Whilst we were packing up, amongst other comments, which I cannot print, Jenny said to me " I thought that baby was never going to cry". I replied, " So did I. Till I pinched it ". Jenny stopped and looked up. " You didn't? - Did You? - No? - Really did you? "

To this day when we are together with friends and this story comes out Jenny asks the same question, but she will have to wait for her answer until on my deathbed with my last gasping breath I will speak the word Yes or No.

Santa is a great gig. When we finished on Christmas Eve I got to take all the presents, which were left, and in costume I put piles of them on the doorsteps of the lone mothers I knew. Sam had more pencils and rulers than she would ever use during her school years, and I got loads of hugs and kiss' from women who would never normally look at a fat man.

That was over fifteen years ago.

Now here's a more recent Santa story, which highlights my tendency even now to snap into man-mode, even when I know better:

My Company was running the entertainment for themed Christmas dinners, which catered for seven hundred people a night. Each day I left home at 11am and drove the seventy miles to our evening venue, returning home about 3-30 am the next morning.

I was offered a job playing Santa for one hour in the afternoon at a hotel about ten minutes from my evening venue. So the £200 fee seemed like easy money.

My agent phoned me a couple of days before to tell me I must have black Wellington boots. " But I use black leather boots. " I said. He insisted that I needed Wellingtons, so at 3-30am when I got home, I painted my blue Wellingtons with black gloss. It was then that I realised I had the next night off. Instead of having a lie in, I'd have to leave earlier than usual and drive to within ten miles of a place I didn't need to go to that day, in order to play Santa.

When I came to leave home seven hours later at 10-30 am, my Wellington boots were still tacky, so I put them in a bin liner and set off on my two-hour journey to the hotel.

The traffic was heavy and I arrived about 1pm. My contact was a young woman called Suzy, and eventually I found her in the function room surrounded by lighting technicians and props people. They were dressing the room just like the North Pole. Gobo lighting, fake snow, sleigh, Christmas trees, wind machine, the lot.

Suzy told me that it was the lady's dearest wish to take her 6-year-old daughter to Lapland but she couldn't make the journey because she was to ill. Having just read an article about how bad the Santa's are in Lapland, I assured her I would do everything I could to give them a great time .The man with the real reindeer arrived and I was informed that I won't be needed until after 3-30pm so one of the hotel staff is asked to allocate me a room.

Being completely ignored by the East European receptionist, who spoke little or no English, I sat down and read the Chat magazine I'd brought with me.

After sitting in reception for 35 minutes doing my crossword Suzy passes by and asks" Haven't they given you a room yet?" She harasses the receptionist who throws me a key " Room 8 " she says pointing to the stairs. I picked up my suit bag and bin liner before climbing the stairs to find my room. It's a single box room overlooking the entrance.

The décor is beige including the carpet, whilst the reproduction Edwardian furniture makes the room feel decidedly tacky. I turned on all the lights and the room still seemed dark. First stop the en-suite. I sit looking around the small room and notice that the wallpaper is peeling at the corners and the newly fitted wall tiles are not level. I'm glad I haven't paid the £156-00 a night for this room.

Having made myself as comfortable as I could, in my matchbox suite, I decided to put on my costume, make a cup of tea and watch TV until Suzy comes for me. The kids have costumes to put on when they arrive, then they'll have their faces painted before getting fed. So I've got at least an hour before collection. Once suited, I decide to try on the Wellingtons that the agent was so sure I needed. Being careful to see that there was no paint on the soles I put on one of the still tacky boots. As I place my foot onto the carpet the boot spreads allowing the edge of the paint to make contact with the beige flooring.

"O shit. I've got black paint on the carpet".
Staggering around a bit my boot touches the floor twice more, before I fall onto the bed.

Subduing my panic by using my newly found Tai Chi,
I remove the boot and throw it back into the bin liner.
Sitting heavily into the lone chair, next to the bed. I
think for a moment. What shall I do? Try as I do, I
can't stop myself going into Man Mode. With my
hand wrapped in toilet paper I start to rub at the paint,
thinking "Don't do it you prat". But it's too late the
thumbnail size black spots are now a group of golf
ball sized black smudges.

OK lets find something to disguise the marks. I know,
coffee creamer, every hotel room has some.

Tipping out the bowl containing tea bags, coffee, and
sugar, white and brown. There it is Creamer. I ripped
open the sachet and poured it onto the paint. Now I
have a carpet covered in a black paste. Half a role of
toilet tissue later I sit looking at the ever-growing
stain on the carpet. Please God I do believe in you.
Please just make the paint disappear. He answers in
the usual way and I try desperately to be sensible.
Deep breaths. Concentrate. My gaze stops on the
packet of aspirins that has fallen out of my suit bag. A
few seconds later I am on my knees with a spoon full
of crushed aspirin powder blowing it onto the stain.
Suddenly I hear someone outside.

If they should enter what will they find? Here is a
man dressed as Santa, kneeling next to the bed
blowing on a spoon full of white powder. Did I lock
the door? I leaped up to make sure, just as the
footsteps passed by.

What now? Once again I sit on the chair, feeling sick
and panic filled. I put on the kettle and make a cup of
coffee.

Then I have another idea. Deodorant goes white when
it dries. Whilst watching the Railway Children and

drinking my coffee, I spray deodorant on the now 12 inch diameter stain, at one minute intervals.

After using up the whole can the patch does look a little lighter? Or is it just wishful thinking.

Suzy collects me at 4-30 pm. I sit in the sleigh and do my best Santa impression for about 40 minutes. The children are led back to the party room and Suzy says, " I'll come up and see you before you go ". I got changed and sat in the room until 6 pm. Its two hours drive home, so I'm not waiting any longer. Placing the chair over what now looks like a dark stain. I turn off the lights and return the key on my way out. I felt guilty but tomorrow is another day. I'm sure things will be better after an early night.

The next day as I sat at the side of the stage my mobile rang. I knew from the displayed number that it was my agent. " Hi Mike, " I say in a cheerful voice, Fully expecting an explosion of abuse and a bill for the carpet. But his reply was completely un expected " I've just had Suzy on the phone. She says you were great, and you're the best Santa they've ever seen. Well-done mate. Cheque'll be in the post in a couple of weeks".

Words for a widow

I have never left you
I'm just in another room
The train I caught was early
So I had to move on through
I will watch and wait until it's time
For you to follow me
Then we can be together for all
eternity
I have never left you
I am safe within your heart
Our love goes on with every beat
Joining us whilst were apart
The memories of happy times
Will always come to mind
Till we can be united and together
for all time
I have never left you
When you need me I'll be there
I'm just around the corner
Sitting in my favourite chair
You will hear my voice upon the wind
You'll feel me by your side
Together we will travel on
In heart and soul and mind

I wrote this poem for a widow I didn't know very
well; I'd only met her husband once at a bar-b-cue.

He seemed a nice guy, but sadly before I had time to know him further he died, from a stroke. His widow's grief was so great that watching her grieve hurt me. I remembered how I felt when my friend Ben died and tried to put into words the beliefs I hold in the hope that they would give some comfort.

I never gave her the poem, because on reflection I was afraid that it may hurt her even more, and I will never press my beliefs onto another person.

I've avoided this rhyme until now because I don't know how I can tell any tales with humour, to go with it. So I'll just tell you of some of the people I've known who I hope are waiting for me wherever it is we go after leaving this world.

But first I want to tell you about RAK's. Random Acts of Kindness. Most of us in our own way perform RAK's regularly. I found them when reading a book written by Danny Wallace. He suggests that we should all do something for a stranger every day. His suggestions range from. Shaking hands with a Traffic Warden to giving a party for an old person. I have used his theory to start what I believe are ripples of good fortune, in the belief that if we start enough we can make the world a better place.

I don't do the lottery because I think that at five to eight on a Wednesday or Saturday there are twenty million people all buzzing with expectancy.

Then at five past eight there are nineteen million who are pissed off. Percentage wise to me the negative vibes out weigh the positive.

Now I think the best RAK's are those done for someone who will never know who did them.

For instance: Leave a bar of chocolate on a strangers desk, pay for an extra coffee for the next customer when you leave a café. Or best of all do something nice for someone you dislike.

The people I'm going to tell you about now unknowingly performed thousands of RAK's not even thinking about it, and the first often gave his help freely saying " Any friend of yours is a friend of mine".

My best ever friend Ben was the first to go. I know he wouldn't mind me telling you how, because I'm sure if he knew in advance how his passing would happen, he would have said. " That will do nicely".

Ben had lived alone for some years since his marriage break up way back in our Fairground days. It would seem that we had an adventure almost everyday we spent together. In our business activities we brought and sold items as far reaching as a boat winch (*Which was concreted into the stones on Bognor Beach*) and a car ramp, which we took apart and moved with a Citroen BX.

About two years before he left us Ben met a lady and fell in love, they were married and incredibly happy for their short time together. One night after having dinner out with friends they came home and went to bed- done what comparative newly weds do. Then Ben got up to go to the bathroom, had a heart attack, and died. He was 46 years old.

In keeping with my conditioning as a man, I never showed any emotion, but when alone in my van I spent many hours over the next three or four years, with tears streaming uncontrollably from my eyes.

We had spoken many times of this happening, and we promised each other that if there was as we believed an existence after this one, whichever of us went first would try and bring good fortune to the other. In my younger days I wondered why I had never won the lottery or the pools. But now being much older I realise that money has little to do with good fortune. Ben sits on my shoulder often and I hear him whisper in my ear " Spend half save half" and " Words said in anger can never be taken back".

As far as the saving is concerned I don't take much notice but I know he would forgive me. It has always been my way to befriend or be befriended by those some years older than myself. When I was in my mid twenties I met Cecil who at the time was in his seventies. In the early days of our friendship, he worked for me, four hours a week as my gardener. Knowing nothing about flowers and plants I instructed him to plant things which would come up every year. I told him it was so that " when you're gone I wont have to do the garden".

By the time he was eighty, he had iron brackets strapped to his legs, and I had to adapt his tools so that he could use them without kneeling down.

Cecil had worked for me for about five years, when he told me he didn't want to be paid anymore, because he loved coming to my house. He would pop in most days, and read my paper whilst he consumed a can of lager, which we always had in the fridge for him.

For the next ten years he sat in my workshop and told us stories of his misspent youth as we worked on cars and motorcycles. To my young daughter he was in some part a second granddad, and to customers he was a fixture.

Once I asked him to dig a hole in the garden. Each day he would excavate a small amount of dirt, until after about two weeks he asked, " What are you going to do with this hole?" My answer was brief " When you die, we will just pop you into it". We all had a laugh and Cecil had a beer.

When I say we I have to include my nephew Roger who worked with me at the time. He once put Cecil on a trike and roared around the garden with him clinging on the best he could.

 One morning we left Cecil weeding the garden. Returning after about half an hour we saw the old fella lying stretched out along the edge of the garden. Roger leapt from the passenger seat even before the car had come to a stop. Shouting " Cecil are you OK". Without moving his body Cecil replied " Its Ok. I got down to pull out some weeds and I couldn't get up, so I just pulled myself along and waited here at the end for you to come back". We gave him a beer, put the kettle on and laughed about it.

Cecil stayed around until he was 91. I kept his car going until he was 90 and after having a succession of minor accidents I convinced him to give up driving. Promising to collect him and bring him to my house after dropping Sam off to school. I was sad when Cecil left us, but I feel better believing that he no longer wears the leg brace and can feel young and useful again.

I suppose the sad thing about getting older is watching those you have known and grown up with go before you.

I have always enjoyed the council of my older friends, and I hope by making new friends, as often as possible I too will have young company as I reach old age. Who was it said, " A stranger is just a friend you haven't met yet"?

In most cases I think very true sentiment.

Another of my older friends was Basil. He was a dumpy old man. With horn-rimmed glasses held together at the bridge by a plaster. At the age of seventy-five his woolly hat covered a full head of hair. He always wore the same old tweed jacket and the zip on his trousers was broken. Whilst I mended his car he'd tell me stories of when he was a drayman. Before meeting him I had no idea that a drayman was a beer deliveryman.

I could see that Basil must have been very strong in his younger days, but now he walked with bowed legs from the weight of the barrels, and of course from riding horses.

Each morning he'd walk past my house to buy a paper and the days food shopping. If I was in the workshop he'd pop in and say hello. Sometimes he would stay a while and chat, others he would say " Must get home to look after the wife". Basil preceded my friendship with Cecil by about five years. Both were always happy and cheerful. Never moaning about money or illness even though neither had much money and both were in bad health.

One morning when I was about 26 Basil came round looking very sad. I made him a cup of tea and asked, " What's up Basil?" His story took me by surprise. He told me that he had joined the army in 1916 and was sent to the trenches during the First World War, and given a rifle.

His superiors told him to shoot and kill any German soldier coming toward them. He said that if any of the English soldiers refused to do this, their own superiors would shoot them. So he had as a boy of 15 shot and killed an unknown number of men.

Each year on poppy day he was reminded of his actions during the Great War, and as he got older his conscience weighed heavy. He was afraid that when he died he wouldn't go to Heaven.

I wanted to say something that would help, but I was just a kid myself and the most violent thing I had ever encountered was a punch in the face. After a few minutes I told Basil that I thought he would be exempt from blame as it was his superiors who told him to do what he did, under threat himself. I drew a picture in his mind of the angels watching with tears in their eyes as so many were killed and mutilated during the confusion of the battle. Those who committed these atrocities with malice or for thought would be the ones remembered and they would have the mark against them in their book of life.

He told me some time later that he felt a little better, but on that day each year the memories of that time would weigh heavy on his conscience.

Basil was the local water bailiff and every day that would allow, accompanied by his good friend Wiz. He would go to the lakes fishing.

One day after waving to them both as they passed my house I went to see my father. He had just retired from the railway and was throwing out his old uniform trousers.

I remembered Basil's trousers with the broken zip. I put the bag of clothes into the boot of my car and thought they would be just the things for Basil when he got home that evening.

I forgot about the trousers for a couple of days until I went to the boot for something. On seeing the bag I drove straight round to Basils house.

The door was opened by his wife *(whom I had never met)*. " Hi I've brought these round for Basil," I said. She was silent for a few seconds before saying " You must be Pip".

I was smiling as I said, " Yes, sorry Basil often talks about you". I dropped the bin liner full of trousers on the step and held out my hand. As she took hold it was not a handshake but more a grip of consolement. " **I'm afraid Basil died yesterday afternoon** ".

Like many times before my foot was firmly stuck in my mouth. I managed to bumble through the following ten minutes as she told me how without Basil she would have to go into a home. She walked with crutches and had little use of her hands. Yet still she was more acceptant of her situation than I was.

The next day I spoke to Wiz who told me this story.

Basil and Wiz had been fishing on opposite sides of the lake. As Wiz was pouring himself a cup of tea from his flask and looked over to Basil, signing do you want a cup. Basil didn't move and appeared to be asleep in his chair. Wiz saw the end of Basils rod bobbing up and down and walked round the lake to wake him up. Obviously Basil was not asleep. He had passed away whilst fishing.

I often imagine Basil fishing, whilst Cecil potters around gardening and Ben entertains them with his get rich quick schemes and words of wisdom.

Many others I have known have joined them. Each passing friend leaving with me an impression, which adds to the value of my life.

I hope I am a culmination of those I have known and the wisdom they have shared with me and I hope I add my own experience to the things I pass on to those new friends I will meet tomorrow.

I choose to believe that this life is just the preparation for something much better, and if I am wrong. Has that belief made me any worse a person?

Friends

Who knows to what depth friendship
reaches.
What lessons of humanity it teaches.
Why bonds are formed in unlikely
alliance.
When time is shared in natural
compliance.

These questions asked need no address.
For friendship shared brings happiness.
It breeds benevolence contentment and
security.
Without thought for race sex or
gratuity.

Good friends listen support and share.
When times are hard they will be there.
So with no negative or tactile face.
Friendship goes beyond this earthly
place.

**" You need not search for those who will be true
friends for they are lead by destiny to find you ".**

Friends have been my saviours time and time again throughout this life. You've been introduced to some of them in previous stories, but as I look back I realise that those who have stayed beside me on my strange and changing road of life, often come from backgrounds and cultures which are far removed from my own. Yet they have offered me help and support in all and any way that they were able, and I would do the same in return for any of them.

My good friends come from both genders, and I seem to have an ability, (*I think is rare in men*), which enables me to have a deep feeling and in fact love for my female friends, whilst not wanting to have sex with them. In fact on many occasions I have told a woman friend to go and put some clothes on.

My friendships with women do however cause a problem when either one of us gets a new partner. Both men and women seem unable to accept that friendship between genders can exist without a sexual element.

I wrote the poem *Friends* when I was thinking about my little friend Hillary. She was only eighteen when I met her, and used to deliver car spares to my garage. Her appearance and manner are so much in opposition, that most men treated her just as a dumb blond. Our Hilly is on face a most beautiful, petite, blond. With a vocabulary which would make many men blush. She can hold her own with the most lecherous and coarse of my gender.

Whenever Hilly came we put the kettle on and often she would stay telling us stories of the men in other garages until her boss phoned me to see where she was. She has been a friend of mine now for nearly fifteen years.

Her partners rarely understand our friendship, and when she works for me in our Circus, she lives in my caravan, where she can wear her pink tracksuit and fluffy slippers, and if she's had a bad day we have a cuddle and a cup of tea whilst she moans about everything that upsets her. We talk about flowers and plants, and the stupid things we do in private. She once told me how she started to eat a bar of chocolate in bed and fell asleep, on waking up she had rolled onto it and when finding the chocolate spread all down her leg thought that she has messed herself. I in turn told her how I did. We laugh together and at each other, and when things are bad for one of us, the other will be there for support. That is friendship.

I had a friend who taught me everything I knew, about business, behaviour, money, and friendship. He is worth a whole book, and when he died at the age of 46. I would often think of him and our many adventures, whilst I sat alone in my car and cried. He was gone before my divorce but I know he would have been there for me and I hope he would be proud of my efforts to live up to his example. His name was Ben Sharp.

I met Ben when I was nineteen; I had finished my apprenticeship as a motor mechanic and went to work on a fairground as a maintenance engineer. Ben was a machine mechanic for a rival firm, but unlike the scruffy young blokes who normally done that job. He always wore a shirt and tie, he was polite to everyone, and always fair to the kids that tried every way they could to fiddle the machines.

In my second year there I managed to talk the site manager into letting me a space to put in a ride, and with support from my father who stood guarantor for my bank loan, I purchased a Ladybird roundabout. The deal I had for payment of rent was that I would pay £200 before Easter, £200 after Easter, £200 a month later, and £200 on August Bank Holiday. I made the first two payments, but was short for the third. Ben and I often had a drink together after work. He had a reputation for being mean, but I later found out he kept a one pound note in his right pocket, a five pound note in his left pocket, and two hundred quid in his back pocket. So that if anyone asked to borrow money, he could show a pound or a fiver and claim to have no money spare.

When he asked me how things were going I told him that I wasn't going to be able to pay my rent. He put his hand into his back pocket and gave me £200 saying " Use that and pay me back when you can ". I asked him why he would lend me money and no one else. He just replied " You're OK". I paid him back mid season and although he asked for no interest I gave him a tenner extra. Later he told me that the extra tenner was one of the things that showed I was a decent bloke.

One of the best things he taught me was: When you meet someone new in a group, Have a plate with an odd number of biscuits, cakes, or sandwiches. Watch to see who takes the most, or if they ask if anyone else wants the last one, and if anyone takes the empty plate back to the sink or counter if in a café.

These things show basic faults in a person and for him made the difference between having a deal or walking away.

I've used this method to note those who are selfish and uncaring ever since, it works every time.

Ben wasn't a walkover. He got the nickname Chainsaw Ben after a car dealer reneged on a payment to us. Ben and I drove to the car sales yard where this particular man had his office. Opening the boot of our car Ben took out a chainsaw walked into the office and asked for the money. Receiving no sensible reply he lifted up the chainsaw, pulled on the cord, which surprisingly caused it to start first time, Then he cut the desk in half right between the mans legs.

Trembling and shouting something like " You fucking mad bastard" he handed over the five hundred quid he owed us. I never saw Ben get mad or raise his voice. I never saw him hit anyone or make a threat.

That story made sure that no one messed with either of us for a very long time.

In the early days of our friendship Ben was married with two young children. He worked in the amusement arcade but was also a chimney sweep, collected scrap metal, and would buy and sell just about anything. One day his wife decided that she didn't want to be with him anymore. So he brought her out of the house and kept the kids for a while. Then for reasons I don't know she had them back. I never saw any aggression in Ben over this, and I remember once helping him to take out his own washing machine and deliver it to his ex wife because hers had broken and he wanted her to be able to wash the kids clothes.

I knew Ben well, we talked about everything, including things men don't normally discuss, and his generosity to family and friends was no act. He genuinely wanted to do the best he could for anyone.

He even gave up his independence to live with his old mum whilst she was dying.

Now you can see what a great guy he was I will tell you what a prat he was as well. Ben decided that as he was living on his own he would buy a house and do it up. He could live in the mess now he didn't have the kids, and when finished he would sell up and move on. The first house he purchased was a small terraced cottage in Littlehampton. The front door opened almost from the street into the lounge, which was 11' 6" wide, and about the same in length. To the left of the room was a small door about 5' high and 18" wide. Inside this door was the smallest staircase I have ever seen. In fact it was so small that neither of us could comfortably walk up it. The stairs led straight into bedroom number one, and across the room another door led into bedroom number two. Downstairs a door led through to the kitchen, which was about 8' deep and then out of the back door was a building with an asbestos roof, which housed a toilet, and the oldest bath I had ever seen. Ben paid £12,000 for this shoebox.

The first thing to do was to open up the two down stairs rooms. Ben was in his early thirties and I was just nineteen, so we didn't need to ask anyone how to do it. With the use of a sledge hammer and a chisel we smashed a hole in the wall and proceeded to take out bricks until his Mk3 Cortina estate was full, then we would go to the tip and empty it, each time returning to make the hole a bit bigger.

After about two days one of Ben's relatives came round, (He was a builder). " Why haven't you put any acro's in yet?" he asked. "Uhh" we replied. We were then given a lecture on how you have prop up the ceiling before you remove the wall. He lent us some acro jacks and helped to install them.

Before he left he informed us that we would need to put in an RSJ girder before removing the acro's.

Now it was my turn for a brain wave. My dad was a train driver and in the old goods yard next to Bognor railway station was a pile of sleepers and train rails. My dad could buy one for us and we would use it to prop up the ceiling, saving a load of money.

In due course, with the help of my father we purchased a length of train track for thirty bob. £1-50. We borrowed a truck and set off to collect the rail. What we didn't know was that train tracks are made of very good quality hardened steel, which weighs considerably more than an RSJ. Ben had to pay six blokes ten bob each to help us load the rail. We did have the sense to realise that the hacksaw we had hoped to use to cut the rail, wouldn't do the job. So off to the local scrap yard we drove. Ten quid and an hour later our rail had been cut to length and we sat outside the cottage wondering how to get it into place on the slightly wobbly brick piers we had built.

The next day with the help of another motley crew and ten bob we got the rail into place

Using a trolley jack and a porta power along with various lengths of timber and some bricks.

With the wall removed we set about the stairs. Ben decided that they should be open plan.

So we ripped off all the cladding and the door. With the wall gone the down stairs was starting to look lighter and bigger.

Ben walked to the bottom step and started to run up the stairs. As he ran up he seemed to be standing in the same spot.

That was because the stairs collapsed and left a hole in the floor where the joists should have been.

After a couple of cups of tea Ben decided to purchase a ready made set of stairs for £125.00. All that remained was the hole in the floor. Rather than remove all the floorboards and fit new joists, we came up with a plan to make a concrete pad for the stairs to sit on. Several barrow loads of concrete later we had a level pad where once a hole had been. The stairs were fitted and seemed to do their job well. Next we decided that as the room was so small it would help if the chimneys were removed. After some thought we decided to knock them down from the upstairs bedroom, and throw the bricks down the chimney into the room below, where just as before we would load them into Ben's car and take them up the tip. I began merrily smashing out bricks. Taking them first from the highest point of the ceiling and working my way down the wall. Once I had taken down the whole of the upstairs I moved to the living room where I carried on working from top to bottom.

Suddenly smoke started to fill the room. I ran upstairs to find smoke bellowing from the hole in the ceiling where the chimney had been. Being bright fellows Ben and I worked out that the chimney in our house must be somehow joined to the one next door, and they had lit a fire. He climbed into the loft to find that there was about ten feet of chimney left on our side and it had developed a two-inch wide crack. With the aid of the two acro's, which were still downstairs we placed a thick piece of wood under the now exposed base of the chimney and across the ceiling joists. We then filled up the cracks with a gunge called mastic. It held back the smoke and the crack got no bigger.

With the fireplace removed we were left with an un plastered wall which was one inch further back than the kitchen one. We found a new type of plaster High Build, which we applied to a depth that brought both walls level. Not knowing how to plaster we couldn't make it smooth. So we drew a pattern in it with the aid of a wooden fan. With the whole lot painted white, we had yet another feature.

By removing the downstairs wall we had created a room twenty-four feet long by eleven feet wide. Sadly we now had no kitchen. So a breakfast bar was cut from a piece of marine ply, and installed parallel to the rear window about five feet into the room. It doesn't take much working out that the kitchen area was now five feet deep by six feet long. Allowing for the stairs and a small walk way to the back door. We called this a Galley feature (as in boat kitchen). Someone had already put in a door leading to the out building, which was made up of a single brick wall, and an asbestos sheet roof. We painted the walls; floor and roof, with a black tar like substance called Aqua seal and then put in a plasterboard ceiling, tiled the walls and floor, and installed the cheapest bathroom suite we could buy. Surprisingly my ability to solder car radiators transferred well to plumbing, and the bathroom was leak free (apart from the roof).

After about six months, several blood blisters, a broken toe, the odd visit to the hospital to remove things from our eyes, twisted ankles, and a big row with the man at the dump. The house was ready for sale. The Agents details read something like:

Two-bedroom terrace cottage.

Fully modernised and with many features.

From the well-presented front courtyard, the newly painted front door leads directly into the expanded Lounge dinner and onto the Galley Kitchen.

The feature wall of which has been installed with the latest thermal High build covering,

The lounge dinner leads directly into the newly fitted Galley kitchen, with all utilities within easy reach.

To the rear of the kitchen sits the fully modernised bathroom. Fully tiled and fitted with an above bath shower.

An open plan staircase offers easy access from the lounge to the two relatively spacious upstairs rooms. Which have been recently re-decorated.

Ben's cottage sold to a couple of first time buyers for £24,500. The day of the survey was more than a little tense. But having just read Gale Carnegie's book. How to Make Friends and Influence People. We made the Surveyor welcome, with a cup of tea, whilst his Jensen Interceptor car gave us something to talk about. A couple of scotches later he left with a non-committal smile on his face. The survey did pick up a couple of things, but not those, which we had expected. Ben moved out and we both made an effort not to go near that part of Littlehampton for a long time. Ben did tell me, he heard that the couple had gone on to do a lot more work on the place. But we never saw them again.

The Child in Me

The child in me wants to run and play.
The man will work suppressed all day.
The child wants sweets and buns and
cakes.
The man eats nothing in his breaks.
The child sees mischief to be made.
The man sits sombre firm and brave.
The child is energetic and impulsive.
The man stays safe reliable and
Honest.

On face I am of age and reputation.
Living up to society's expectation.
Inside the child longs to be free he is in
truth a part of me.

The balance is sometimes hard to find.
But both exist in heart and mind.

The child in me is a recent poem. I wrote it after a conversation with a very professional lady who comes from an entirely different background to my own. She sees me in work of a serious and stern nature and once said in a note to me. " I looked in to say hello and there you were, sat looking straight ahead professional as always". I wondered how many people only see the man, and not the child in my heart. In truth it is that part which gives me aspirations to be more understanding of others and try to bring a little fun and happiness to those around me. So, I wrote the poem for all those people who accept too easily the restrictions of age, and I thank that lady for making me realise. I sometimes take things too seriously.

As I reached middle age I tried to be the man I thought society expected me to be, but eventually I came back to the same conclusion I made all those years ago when I wrote *Vocation*. I can only be the man I am, if I try to be someone else I think I will always fail. The years have taught me many lessons, some of them hard and justly so. I have at last learned to let the child in my heart play whilst being protected by the experience of my mind.

Which leads nicely into some of the childish things I have done. You may think that my admissions to being skint most of the time aren't true.

"How could you have done all the things you claim with no money?" I hear you ask. Well as with Roger and the boats, I've been lucky In that those friends I've known since my teenage days have had good fortune in business, and have never forgotten the friend who was there all those years ago.

When they had expensive toys, I was always allowed to play with them. (*So long as I helped mend them when they broke*).

My life swings like a pendulum even to this day, I am never quite sure where the next pound will come from, or if I will fall desperately in love with someone and get recklessly into debt trying to impress her.

In my earlier years the latter wasn't a problem, as after the failure of my marriage I had neither the time nor inclination to have another relationship.

So when Sam was young, during the week I worked from my garage at home as a mechanic, assisted by either a cousin or nephew. Then at weekends and some evenings I added to my income by working as an entertainer. I would also buy and sell anything in which there was a profit.

My turnover was good but never quite met my outgoings. So once a week, on an evening when I wasn't working, (*usually a Friday*) we would have a bar-b-cue or some other low cost do it your-self gathering. Bar-b cues were a favourite, as my cousins, nephews, and friends all had children about the same age. So we would all club in and buy whatever we could afford to cook on the Bar-b.

My next-door neighbour Paul would always bring a crate of beer, and his generosity enabled many of the other guests to wake up the next day with headaches. As engineers we never brought anything we could make, so an old coffee machine was converted into our first bar-b-cue, which lasted about five years and bar-b- ing we went. The evenings themselves would be impromptu and more often than not a ring round at 5 pm would ensure the attendance of anything between fifteen and thirty friends and family, all accompanied by kids.

It was about this time I decided that if there is a God, he ain't gona help me. Whenever I am enjoying myself he pisses on me.

I used to tell Sam that rain was God pissing on us and thunder was him farting. (She's *not afraid of thunder, but is reluctant to go out in the rain*). Hence we vowed to Bar-b whatever the weather.

In the early days we used a large waterproof sheet supplied by one of the builders in our family, to cover the garden. I obtained four five hundred watt floodlights, which doubled as heaters if you sat near them and with the washing line pole stuck in the middle. We had a reasonably dry area. This was great until the sheet filled with water and then at any given moment a deluge would cover whoever was sat near the edge. Often this deluge was directed by one of the other guests who had stood up and hit their head on the now sunken sheet. We later replaced the sheet with a bungalow tent, which we bought second hand for fifteen pounds. It was twenty feet long by fifteen feet wide, and had four rooms and a lounge. The rooms had to be thrown away after a bottle of Coca-Cola exploded and I forgot to wipe the internal covers before packing the tent away. Next time I got it out the inner sheets were rotted away. (*Imagine what Coke must do to your stomach*). The tent lasted about three years during which time the bar-b-cue set fire to it on a regular basis. If it fits with another poem I might tell you about the time we went to the New Forest and woke up with a donkey in the tent. Or Hannah's " turd in the bucket story".

No perhaps I won't!

Before we leave my garden I must tell you about the swimming pool. Sound's grand doesn't it?

When my Sam was about fourteen I was saving up for
a Harley Davidson. My jar contained about three
hundred pounds, and by the March of that year the
sun was shining daily and the long-term weather
forecasts promised a heat wave. So as often happens
with me. We had nothing to do one day, and ended up
in the local garden centre. There in front of us was the
offer we couldn't refuse. A fourteen-foot above
ground swimming pool with filters, for two hundred
and fifty quid. After a very short conversation with
Sam, I decided that it would take forever to save the
other five and a half grand for a Harley. So we
brought a pool.

At the end of my back garden was a raised patio
feature. Made up of fourteen inches of brick rubble
and concrete. This came about during a bedroom
conversion. Ben and I made to my house. (*Having
had plenty of practice on his properties*). We decided
that a skip was too expensive and built the patio, or
concrete slab, whichever you prefer to call it.
Anyway it served ideally as a platform for the
Swimming pool, and by noon the following day there
it was erected and ready to fill. If you get frustrated
watching a kettle boil, try filling a swimming pool. It
took six hours for the hose to transfer two and a half
thousand gallons of water. We would pop out and
have a look about every half hour. It was worse than
waiting for Christmas. Eventually by about seven that
night there was enough water to make the pool stable.
On with our swimming gear and in we went. Hypo-
thermia didn't put us off at all.

The instructions said that we had to wait three days
for the chemical filter to make the water safe, but we
didn't die. It was bloody cold though and Sam had
more friends that summer than ever before.

One night she had about a dozen girls in there.

I found out afterwards that some of them had been drinking wine. They all decided to run from one side to the other as it made the pool wobble. I just stopped them before it collapsed.

During school time my use of the pool was exclusive. I purchased a blow up floating chair for fifty quid and any afternoon that it was sunny. I could be found floating in the pool. I brought some wire hangers from the pound shop, which you put over your radiators to hang clothes on, and adapted them for use as shelves for the side of the pool.

So there I would be. Sandwich and lemonade resting on my, in pool shelf. Then whilst floating in my blow up chair I'd make several calls to my friends who were at work, from my brick mobile phone. Just to say "Guess where I am?"

I often had to fish out soggy sandwiches when they fell into the pool, but the filter seamed to deal well with the spillage of tea or orange juice.

The number of burgers on the bottom of the pool next day assessed the success of a bar-b- cue, and we took bets on how far the cat would get across the cover before it sank.

My fun ended when firstly the cigar I was smoking fell onto the arm of my inflatable chair, causing it to deflate with such speed that I sank complete with mobile phone, sandwich, and drink. Then when I went on holiday my cousin John forgot to turn on the filter and on my return I had a two and a half thousand- gallon pond, complete with frogs. I told him he had to clean off the algae and he decided to do it with a broom. In doing so he made a small hole in the liner, which enabled the chemically enhanced water to leak out and run into the allotments behind my house.

I became afraid to go out in my garden that summer as all I could hear were angry voices coming from the allotment holders, debating why their vegetables had all suddenly died. By the end of the next year we had had enough of the pool and I gave it to a friend in Bournemouth whose kids enjoyed it for several years. Not bad for two hundred and fifty quid.

We didn't always bar-b-cue. One Friday I told everyone to dress up in his or her best clothes and I'd take them out to dinner. At 7pm in convoy I led them all to Tescos where the café had an offer on Curry nights, £3-50 per person. The women in the café thought we were mad, but joined in with our fun, as did any late shoppers who came in. Another time I took everyone to Smart Tony's Sherpa van parked in a lay by on the A27. "As much as you can eat and I'll pay for it". Was my cry!
Smart Tony was a Turk and complete with Classic Cigar, he would serve up the biggest bacon or burger roles you've ever seen. Loading them with extra grated cheese, and occasionally cigar ash.
He'd just keep them coming until no one could eat any more. Then when it came to paying, *(because my nephew had once helped him by replacing a fuse in his van when he broke down)*. Tony would say, " Just call it a fiver".
I can't leave *the child in my heart* without telling you about the Blues Brothers outing.
To me and I am sure my nephew Roger it was just another night with the kids. But to my Sam it must have been special as she often mentions it when talking to her friends

Roger's wife worked nights and so we'd take his two littlies, Scot and Hannah, plus my Sam, and do something fun. We'd been going to the amusements at Hayling Island, where we'd give the kids five quid each and tell them to loose it as fast as possible. Roger had a foolproof system for emptying the pushers and within half an hour we'd have all the prizes and handfuls of ten pence's. His son Scott was a wiz with fruit machines and came out with at least double his money. Roger would then spend a couple of quid and win a carrier bag full of cuddly toys for the girls, then the bloke who owned the place would kick us out. My favourite moment was when we left. We would look for some kid who was with a mean parent. You know Dad stands there playing the machine whilst the kid just watches. We'd give the kid all our copper and say " Don't take money from strangers unless your Dad's with you".

After a while we felt sorry for the amusement owner so we decided to dress up as the Blues Brothers and make our own fun. First stop was the Black Horse. This was one of the first restaurant/ pubs and was making a name for its food, which attracted a wealthy and middle classed cliental. There were a few funny looks as we ordered our drinks complete with black trilby hats and sunglass. Someone tried to start a conversation with me about cricket, so in character I announced that all cricketers were nonses and we started singing Raw Hide.

No one joined in so we went into the garden to play with the kids. It just so happened that another of my friend's daughters, whose name was Mandy worked in the restaurant, so I decided to go and say hello. Now Mandy was a delightful young woman. Beautiful, blond, intelligent and gentle.

I could see her embarrassment at having to talk to me, but I had an on going game of lets embarrass Mandy going with her Step Dad. So before leaving I said very loudly. "See you later Mandy, don't forget. Bring the dirtiest friend you've got. 11 o'clock room six, and there's an extra hundred for you". She just looked at the floor and went into the kitchen. (*I am so sorry Mandy*).

Next we went to another pub called the Tram. Roger was into photography so we took a camera wherever we went. This night we took a video and went around interviewing people in the bar. We got some to sing for us and were having a great laugh with everyone. We had a count up and decided we had just enough money to order some food. The kids were playing happily in the garden. So Roger and I continued to have a laugh with the waitress. I noticed one of them come out of the kitchen crying and wondered if it was anything to do with us. So I took off my hat and glasses and wandered over. " I'm sorry if we've done anything to upset you. I know were a bit loud but we're just having a laugh ". She said that it was nothing we'd done, but the chef was a nasty piece of work and had sworn at her when she ordered our food. I walked into the kitchen and shouted " Which one of you ignorant bastards has just Sworn at this little girl?" The biggest, ugliest, unshaven brute stepped forward saying. " It was me! Who the fuck do you think you are?" (*O' Shit I thought*).

Looking round I saw the deep fat fryer bubbling away next to me and in my best calm threatening voice I said " Come here" waving a finger as I spoke. The chef came to about six inches from my face.

Using my best acting skills I said in a soft and
threatening voice " If the next word from your mouth
isn't Sorry to this kid. I'll take your right hand and
immerse it in this deep fat fryer". The widening of my
eyes must have done it because he backed away,
As he did so he turned to the waitress and said, " I
didn't mean to upset you, I'm a chef, we get stressed".
I went back into the bar and sat next to Roger saying,
" I think we'd better leave before the police get here".
But before we could go the girl came over and hugged
me.
Every other drink that night was free. Even the chef
came out and joined in after his shift. We met a three-
piece band that were on their way home after a double
booked gig and we all had a sing song in the car park.
It may sound as if I was something of a thug, but in
my defence. I haven't drunk alcohol since the late
seventies, and all of the acts committed by the Child
in my Heart are just that. Childish fun.

Love of my Life

She is a thing of beauty, rounded and
smooth.
Motionless and silent, awaiting my
return.
Those passing admire her sculpted
curves.
And dream of seeing,
that which is hidden from sight.

When we're alone I sink deep into her,
and together we roll from left to right.
Joined as one, holding tight.
Working in harmony to achieve
our mutual satisfaction.

When still, she purrs with gentle
regularity.
Poised and ready for sudden excitement.
And when she sleeps
I gently lay the cover over her
perfectly formed and voluptuous body.

Sometimes in Spring I watch her from a
distance.
As she stands majestic in the park.
Whilst those around fade into obscurity.
Silent and still her magnetic charm
exudes,

to envelope those who glance her way.
Stealing a smile from hearts,
some cold as the frozen dew.

They wish that she was theirs ,
and dreams exotic run through their
wandering minds.
But I am solid in the knowledge, that she
is mine.

In summer she is sleek and fast.
Moving with subtle grace.
The breeze passes over her undulating
form,
Whilst the sun 's soothing rays
 change the colour of her olive body.

In autumn the sound of her is like music.
When it is blended with the rustling of
dry fallen leaves,
Being blown by the reaping winds.
Softly I place upon her an extra
covering.
The intimate bond between us,
growing with each movement of my
massaging hand.

With the arrival of winter,
She will stay safe in the confines of our
home.
Still and silent, she stands admired like
art.
Shimmering light reflecting from her
motionless form,
As the fading sun drops below the
window,
and is replaced by the blue tinted beams
of the moon.

It is this time which is the best between
us.
No prying eyes. No lusting glances.
She is mine and mine alone.
I can pamper her. I can love her.
I can spend the long winter nights
looking at her.

And then with the coming of spring
We will drive out together,
And everyone will see.
The pride and love I have
For my 1966 three point eight
S type Jag.

I think that for us men, or at least for me, it is
sometimes easier to love a vehicle than a woman.
A car is an animate object. It can stimulate and be part
of the greatest thrills. It can visually impress and
bring power. It has no opinions.
I admit a vehicle lacks the tactility and softness of a
woman, but with a mechanical object, I am not
continually afraid of doing the wrong thing.
I was once talking to a lovely young woman, who had
a child by a particularly nasty man and was having
trouble getting rid of him. I asked her why she went
with him in the first place and she replied, " Because
he had a Toyota Hi Ace".
The poem *Love of My Life* is really a joke. I did once
own a 3.8 s type jag, and it was a beauty. Deep Red
with a gold pin stripe and 10-inch chrome Dunlop
wheels. I can still smell the leather interior and the
walnut dash. I was eighteen when I owned that car
and it cost me almost all of my earnings to run it. My
cousins and nephews certainly had fun with their
girlfriends, in the back. But I was just interested in
driving the car. Here is how my love affair with
vehicles started.

In 1970 Rock and Roll was still a strong force in the
musical culture of youth. I played my guitar in the
youth clubs strumming hits from Donovan and Jim
Reeves. I rode as pillion on Triumph Bonneville's and
Norton Commando's, which dripped a pint of oil from
their crankcases for every gallon of petrol burnt.

At the age of fourteen the speeds of sixty or seventy miles an hour (*often proclaimed to be ninety to a ton*) seemed like the speed of light, at a hundred miles an hour your eyelids fluttered un controllably and when a fly coming in the opposite direction emptied the contents of it's body into your eye. It took about two hours for the bits to wash out or get sniffed down your throat.

I spent many an evening as a pillion on some motorcycle cruising between Bognor Regis and Worthing sea fronts, looking for Parker clad Scooter riders, to whom we would stick up two fingers or shout abuse as we rode by. This would in the retelling become a mass punch up with blood and guts left all over the road.

In fact it was more likely that on the way home someone would get a puncture or break down and most of our time was spent trying to get a rubber patch to stick to an inner tube in the rain. I found it easy to get a lift on the outward journeys but if the driver happened to meet a girl whilst at our destination, I, along with any other male pillion passengers might find we were walking home.

By day I was a quiet stocky boy who done just enough work not to be noticed as he sat in the back of the class. Anonymous to everyone but the PE teacher who took great pleasure in ridiculing the" fat boy" and making him stumble round the outskirts of the playing field.

By night I wore a black leather jacket emblazoned with a black and white swastika bearing the words " Rat Fink ". The older boys I mixed with at night were much kinder to me than those at school (*Once I had passed all of the initiations*).

One of which included attempting to bite off a chicken's head (*It was Dead*). My biker friends were like family to me.

The hierarchy of the group started at the top with the one who had the fastest bike, and worked down to the wannabees like me. If you knew your place and gave the respect to those above you, the group was kind and benevolent to all members.

I had little money but hardly ever needed to buy a drink. In the grown up world outside of school my friends never allowed me to be bullied. With my mediocre skill on the guitar, and ability to make up instant songs of dubious quality. I was the biker's minstrel.

Half way through my fourteenth year I became the target of the school bully (*Mainly by jibes and threats*). Probably because I didn't react to them he decided to escalate his harassment by hitting me in the face.

As he was doing this I realised that it didn't really hurt that much and putting down my Gladstone style brief case. I stood firm and punched him straight on the nose as hard as I could. His nose burst as he fell backwards onto the tarmac in silence. In a mater of seconds the group, which up until now had encircled me chanting to the bully "Bash Him Up", completely dissolved. I was left alone with the dazed and bleeding victim of my blow.

Before I could even think about my next action I found myself being dragged by the PE teacher to appear before the Headmaster. Who wasn't interested in why I had hit the boy but simply informed me that my parents would be called to the school in order to consider my punishment?

The next day as I sat before the Headmaster accompanied by my Mum and Dad I couldn't bring myself to tell in front of my father, that for most of my school life bullies had called him a Nigger and a Wogg (*words that in today's world would seem more comical than abusive*). My failure to answer the question " Why did you break his nose? " was greeted with the threat of expulsion.

My father never punished me but I could see the disappointment in his eyes. He had wanted me to be a Doctor like the Grandfather I had never known.

I decided that school was an unjust place and I never went back again. Each morning I'd ride my bike to my sister's house near the school and then go to work with a Stock Car racing team I'd met a short while before.

After about two months I returned home to find a truant officer had visited my parents. My father was a good and just man but to disgrace him brought instant punishment. After which we discussed my future. He agreed that as long as I had some sort of qualifications I could follow any career I wished. I chose to be a Motor Mechanic, so my father drew out the endowment policy he had been paying into for my university education and I went motor racing.

My biker friends had connections with a hard man called Jim. He raced a Super Stock car. I started to help along side those who made up his pit crew. Mine were the dirtiest jobs, checking the oil, filling up the petrol, changing tyres, and of course making the tea. It occurred to me that if I made the tea taste awful I wouldn't have to make it any more. So I added a teaspoon of swarfega (*industrial hand cleaner*) to each cup. To my amazement no one noticed.

So I continued to make the tea every day for the next six months.

In order to pacify my father, I agreed to get an apprenticeship in a proper garage and so long as I worked there by day I would be allowed to go racing at night. I got on my pushbike and cycled around the local area until I was taken on by one of the garages. My first week's wages was thirteen pounds and five shillings.

One day a week I attended the local college to obtain a City and Guilds qualification, the cost of which I had to pay from my earnings, sixteen pounds a term. This was because I had left school before taking my O level exams. In fact from that day on I've had to pay for every course and qualification I've ever taken. Repairing the race car or going to the tracks consumed most of my evenings and weekends, and In order to keep my dad happy I always turned up for work on time, even if we'd been working on the race car all night. (*At this time in my life sleep seemed both unnecessary and a complete waste of time*).

The tracks we raced at were spread all across the country from Ipswich to White City and there would often be as many as six people in the tow car. Sometimes if I annoyed them (*usually by passing wind loudly*) the other mechanics would make me sit in the stock car on the trailer as it was towed to the track. The Super-Stox had no windows so it was extremely cold and often wet, but like an idiot I would sit in the drivers seat pretending that I was in some race hanging the back end out as I powered into a corner.

Since my decision not to allow myself to be bullied I'd refused to cry and made a point of telling everyone.

The consequence was the invention of the game "lets make Pip cry". When travelling in the tow car I had to sit in the middle of the back seat and two of the older mechanics who sat either side would take turns in giving me Chinese burns or punching my arm to try and make me cry. If this didn't work they'd give me horse bites, a sort of full-handed pinch. I was bruised all over my thighs and arms but never cried.

The fact that I feel I have to tell you I never cried is another example of the man in me, and just one of the things I feel I have to ask forgiveness for. It is my dearest dream that one day I will be able to shed a tear without embarrassment or threat to my masculinity.

The games stopped when whilst I was welding the chassis of the race car one night Jim *(who called me Rat Fink because of the insignia on my leather jacket)* kept making fun of me. I can't even remember what he was saying but in the uncontrolled temper of my youth I turned towards him hot welding rod in hand and thrust it into his arm. He could easily have beaten me to a pulp but he just walked off and never spoke of it again.

Looking back it seems that it was about then I became accepted as part of the team. Still only fifteen years old I relied on the older boys in the race team to protect me from other mechanics at the racetracks who were less tolerant. My cheek to them would be dealt with by a punch in the arm but if any outsider picked on me they would defend my honour ferociously. The aggression of the track would carry on into the pits and often a mechanic would go home with as many bumps and scratches as the car.

Things, which today would be seen as cruel or illegal, were in fact considered only the initiation of a boy into a Mans World. I was in no way innocent. My favourite trick was to empty the contents of a red-X can down the crack of someone's backside. I even swapped the wires on the plug of a drill so that one of the others got an electric shock, and I once put tobacco in a blokes sandwiches, and pissed in half a bottle of scotch which was consumed a day later by the whole team. (*Except me because they said I was too young to drink*). The friends I made during those early race days have stayed around and some are still there for me today.

So for two years by day I learned about engines and repaired cars. By night I travelled the country with a group of adrenalin junkies. At the time of my fifteenth birthday I was about twelve stone and had red sores around my mouth from eating sandwiches with greasy hands. In fact even after being washed, my hands still had black streaks embedded into my skin and that was the cleanest part of me. Deodorant for men hadn't been invented and I was sure my body was allergic to soap.

The best present I got that year was my yellow overalls with a blue stripe down the side. Dressed in these I would now have free access to all areas.
I can't remember how, but I met a girl called Linda at White City stadium .I do remember the first time I kissed her. It was a bit like sucking raw squid only more slimy. I was disappointed until I noticed the other guys watching who proceeded to give us a round of applause " Now I'm a man " I thought or something like that.

I wrote to Linda two or three times a week for about three months. I even wrote her poems and songs and if I remember correctly sent her a red rose in a plastic container. It never seemed odd that she ran the Derry Warwick fan club. (*Yes the same Derry Warwick who later became a champion formula 3 driver*). Until someone told me that she had been paid by Jim's race team to pretend to be my girlfriend.

It was around this time the first British Demolition Darby was to be held at Aldershot stadium, which was our local track. Jim knew well my desire to drive a car so he entered an Austin A55 for me. He lied about my age and brought me a race licence.
The whole team helped to prepare the car. Ripping out the windows and upholstery and fitting a piece of four by four wood behind the drivers seat, in case the car rolled over. Our version of a full harness seat belt was an old parachute harness from World War 2. Once strapped into the car I could hardly see over the steering wheel. In fact I could only just reach the pedals and couldn't have fully depressed the clutch or brake pedal, even if I had time to. I drove jerkily onto the track and took my place half way down the grid. The Commentator at the time was a man called Nigel King. He was introducing the line up and psyching up the crowd, when I noticed someone painting words on the side of my car. "One hundred cars in a race to the death" I heard him say. The painter disappeared and I suddenly realised the seriousness of my situation. I remember well the noise of the revving engines and the smell of burning oil. I don't remember letting up the clutch or turning the steering wheel as I was pushed around the track from behind, sometimes-on two wheels.

I had no control whatsoever over the vehicle whilst it was rammed from back front and all sides. Eventually after about five minutes the car with me inside was beaten into a cube shape and pushed hard into the fence. All I could see was the steam spraying from what was once a radiator and a marshal jumping up and down with a yellow warning flag, which no one was taking any notice of. I could hear screeching as the wheels of the car behind span on the tar-mac, whilst trying to ram me further into the crash barriers. It's unlikely I had completed more that a couple of laps and none of it under my own steam. In fear I released the parachute harness and climbed through the hole where once had been the windscreen.

As I stood on the bonnet a car headed straight for me. The next thing I knew I'd jumped over the barrier and was laying in the crowd, less a fingernail.

It later turned out that the phantom painter, who had appeared at the start, was in fact playing a practical joke. Which had lead to my extreme and quick demise. One of the mechanics had painted the words " Nigel King's Lost His Handbag" on my car. Mr King being the commentator had taken offence at this and offered a substantial cash reward to the car that killed me.

I did race in this category once more at the old Cross in Hand track in Arlington. Built on the side of a hill the track was closed in the mid seventies. I went back to look at it a few years ago. The concrete raceway sat cracked by weeds and surrounded by vegetation. No sign of the race control, or the burger bar where I spent many a happy hour. I stood for a moment and was sure that in the wind I could hear the March of the mods music that preceded the start of every race.

The car entered for me at Cross in Hand was an Austin A33. It was about the size of a peanut. The brakes were non-existent and the tyres about 5 inches wide. I made about one and a half laps on the wheels and half a lap on the roof. Jim had a fight with another driver at this track and was banned. So he had to go out with the track owner's daughter for a few months to get his licence back.

I know you'd love to hear the stories of the girls Jim had at every track, but they're not my stories so I won't tell them. For me girls were just a distraction from having fun. If I could have kept that view I would now be much richer and driving an Aston Martin.

Jim was a good driver and certainly up amongst the best dozen in the country. His aggression was well known and few people would approach him after a bad race. One day I made a terrible mistake. It was at the British Super Stox Championships at Ipswich Stadium. Jim had come in the first three in each of the heats and stood a good chance of winning the championship. Such a win would bring him a reasonable amount of money and some possible sponsorship. My job was to fill up the petrol tank which held two gallons of fuel about two thirds of which would be used during the thirty lap race. This was around the time that I had my hired girlfriend Linda and in keeping with a trait I still have today. I was so engrossed talking to her that I forgot to fill up the Super-Stox with fuel.

I wasn't even aware that the cars had gone out to the start line until I heard the engines rev and the roar of the crowd as the race started. I froze for a few seconds realising that Jim didn't have enough fuel for the race.

I watched from the crowd as he drove like a demon passing several cars on each lap. By lap ten he was behind the leader and both fought to retain their places for the next ten. Finally Jim took the lead and continued to race ahead lapping tail-enders.

He was eventually one and a half laps in the lead, when the engine began to splutter. My heart sank. I felt sick. I hid under the stadium seating. Jim coasted along the home straight towards the chequered flag. Those he had lapped passed him on both sides. The second place car caught up and cruised passed about a hundred yards before the end.

I got a lift home with someone else and stayed away from Jim for a week.

The journey to any of the racetracks was always a long and boring one, with a large number of people squeezed inside the old blue Vauxhall, which also had to pull a trailer containing the race car, spare wheels and a boot full of tools. It always seemed like we were working on the car until the last minute, and one Thursday with the meeting starting at 7-00 pm we left for Aldershot about 5. Two miles from home the drop plate (*a thick piece of metal which lowered the height of the tow ball*) snapped. As the Stock Car and trailer came up along side the tow car Jim calmly turned into the trailer and nudged it onto the grass verge slowing it down, as car and trailer came safely to a halt a few yards from a narrow road bridge. We all tumbled out and removed the broken part, adapted the tow ball, hooked up the trailer and continued on to the race, arriving in plenty of time. Luckily for me that wasn't one of the times I was sitting in the stock car.

There were even times when we would stop to repair punctures on the tow car at the side of the road. You can guess who had to inflate them with a foot pump. To pass the time on the journeys which lasted up to five hours. I would make up songs or rhymes. So long as I could keep everyone entertained they didn't play " Lets make Pip cry " or " Lets give Pip horse bites ". On one journey to Lydden Hill race circuit. I told them of a dream I'd had the night before. This is a track built for saloon car racing. The tracks we usually raced on were quarter mile oval. Lydden was a longer track with bends in both directions. Because of the differences the rear axel had to be fitted with an unlocked differential instead of the usual locked one.

This meant that both back wheels could revolve at different speeds; reducing traction and making the car handle very differently. On this occasion we had to use a Differential of a ratio not quite correct for the track.

Anyway from my dream I described the track as going away from the start line which was about two thirds down the straight and into a right hand bend which had red and white crash barriers instead of the usual wire ropes. On the inside of the bend there were stacks of tyres over concrete posts as apposed to the dirt boarder of the oval track. The car became silent as I continued. I later found out that my description of the track I had never seen was considered too accurate to be made up. I continued to tell how in my dream Jim had got off to a good start but struggled to keep up because of the loss of traction caused by the wrong differential. Eventually on lap three he would undertake a risky manoeuvre and roll the car ending up with the car on its roof.

It was almost an honour to race at Lydden Hill Circuit. Stock Cars were only allowed once a year and we were all excited to be there. Jim lined up on the start grid in our freshly painted Team Super Stock. The start was a rolling one. This meant one lap behind a pace car and then as it pulled off and the race began. Jim roared passed a couple of cars and into the first bend but instead of the car rear end drifting pendulous into the correct position to power out. The whole car drifted to the outside of the track and allowed others to pass. I knew how Jim would react to this and watched as he rammed and weaved his way up the straight and into the next bend. Where exactly the same happened.

Over the next two laps Jim fought bravely to gain places on the straight and took greater chances to hold on to them around the corners. Between laps three and four his car rolled ending up on the roof. Jim released his full harness and pulled himself from the car. Standing along side the inverted vehicle he put his hands onto the chassis and appeared to throw the car back onto its wheels. He then took off his helmet and holding it by the strap smashed it through the fibreglass roof before walking off.

I was forbidden to talk about my dreams from that day on. It didn't stop me having them though.

I passed my City and Guilds part 1 and whilst on holiday from work went to do some repairs on a fair ground, the owner of which offered me a job as his engineer. Repairing Roller Coasters seemed much more exciting than cars. So I left the garage where I earned twenty-two pounds a week and joined the fairground on Thirty-two.

My time with Jim and the boys ended there. We remained friends but my new job and my Disco now used up all the time I had.

I should explain that throughout my life I have often worked in several different occupations at the same time and as we travel on in my reminiscences you'll find many stories overlap. For instance: during my early days with Jim and the team I somehow found time to play Country music at the local college social club, and along with my cousin Johnny ran a Disco called Close Encounters. But those stories are for another time

My race days continued when I was twenty-four. Now married with three stepchildren. I was running a Car repair workshop from behind my house and Jim would often pop round to borrow welding gas or tools from me. On one of these occasions he had a Mini Hot Rod on his trailer. After some negotiations I purchased it from him for the sum of one hundred and fifty pounds. The Shell was smashed to bits but the running gear, engine and auxiliary parts were good. I spent the next three weeks building the parts into a new body .Of course I had to buy spare wheels, a trailer, overalls, helmet, gloves, fuel cans, and a whole host of extras needed before I was ready to race.

With the summer ahead of us we set off to join the Hot Rod Grass Track set. My wife was never too keen on either the racing or my friends but to be fair she would load up the kids, make a packed lunch, and pile into the car, as I got ready to drag our load to the local racetrack. The format of racing I took part in was a new type concept called Grass Track. Most of the early Hot-Rods racing here were retired cars from the Tar-Mac Oval. We raced in an old abandoned gravel pit.

The spectators stood around the top, which was about fifty foot above the track. This gave a great view of the quarter mile compacted gravel raceway and a degree of safety for them. At this time I weighed about fifteen stone so with the drivers door of my mini hot rod welded shut for safety I had to cut the door skin down by about five inches so that I could get into the car through the expanded window space. Some of the drivers who had money but could not make it on the Tar-Mac Oval had joined our club and brought highly tuned expensive cars.

Along with equally expensive wives. In the hope that they could clean up, and win most of the trophies, which they did.

Sadly those of us who were not as good at driving as they were, kept bumping into their cars and eventually they got all dented and broken. I have to admit I, along with most of the others ran my car on a shoestring. I didn't have time to spray the car so I'd hand paint it. I couldn't afford a rally style role cage so I made mine out of old scaffold pipes welded together and I would always buy the scrutineers a cup of tea so that they'd overlook small safety lapses and let me race.

My wife would dutifully look after the three kids, and make sure they all watched me when my race came up. I in turn would race away from the start line. Overtake a car or two and then hold my own for the rest of the race. I found that if I just stayed in the middle of the pack, those who took the chances in their quest to come first would often crash, blow up their engines, or get smashed by some tail-ender. So more often than not I finished in sixth or seventh place out of twenty starters.

So long as I wasn't the last home I was happy. Well in truth I didn't care if I was the last home. You see I've always been more of a Tortoise than a Hare. I really believe that taking part for the fun of it is good enough. The pit we raced in had cambered walls so once I got going I would allow my car to ride up the wall about fifteen feet. I had learned from my time on the fairgrounds that anything moving faster than forty-five miles an hour would stick to a wall. I once had a go on a wall of death. I shit myself but done it in a clumsy fashion.

Anyway. Whilst everyone else fought for the inside line I would drift to the outside and ride the wall. Then if there was a pile up on the corner. I'd emerge several places nearer the front. This gave me another three laps before everyone overtook me again. I once had a photo of two minis upside down on a bend with me driving over them. Well that's what it looked like. My lateral thinking has worked with varying success throughout the many and varied activities I've undertaken but all good things have to come to an end. These were the days before health and safety became the burdensome animal it is today. My petrol tank was a two-gallon jerry can bolted where the back seat had been. A pipe was brazed into the bottom of the can and rubber hose connected it to an electronic fuel pump mounted alongside. A switch by the driver turned the power to the pump on or off and the whole fuel system was exposed directly to the driver.

One sunny Sunday afternoon during my second season of Mini –Hot Rod racing at my home track of Funtington I was riding the wall as usual. It may be the gravel was wet or I wasn't going fast enough to stick to the wall, but my car ended upside down in the middle of the bend.

The others passing me seemed to be travelling in slow motion as they swerved either side of my upturned car. One hit the rear corner and spun me around to see my wife standing at the top of the pit screaming. As usual I was laughing loudly and watched the marshals jumping up and down waving their yellow flags to warn the other cars to slow down.

I was waiting for the opportunity to exit the vehicle safely, when I noticed the clicking of the fuel pump, its rhythm much faster than normal.

I had an idea then that the plastic union had broken off the fuel pump. This was confirmed when I saw a growing puddle of petrol on the inside of the upturned roof. The first time I hit the quick release full harness safety belt nothing happened. I stopped laughing and hit the belt again several times. As I struggled to try and release myself I noticed the sparks coming from the electric points, which operated the fuel pump. Somehow I managed to take my weight off of the safety belt just long enough to escape. Falling into the puddle, which was growing beneath me. Petrol splashed up into my eyes as I crawled out of the driver's window and onto the track where the marshals guided me to the St Johns ambulance to have my eyes washed out with water.

From crash to exit my ordeal was in reality no more than a minute but to me it seemed like ten. I know you want me to tell you that the car exploded but that wouldn't be true. One of the marshals turned off the power switch and the petrol just ran into the compacted gravel. Thus ended my Hot-Rod Driving days.

My wife whom I loved dearly at the time refused to come to the track any more and although she would never believe it.

I wanted to be with her and the kids more than I wanted to drive a race car. So I looked for other things to fill our weekends. Most of which she wasn't interested in either. I tried Wind Surfing, Boating, and Fishing. We had another baby and then she left me to live with an older man.

It was about this time I met Jimmy M. This Jim was the opposite of my old racing mentor. He was a short stocky man in his late thirties. His job was a strange one.

He worked as a Trouble Shooter for a worldwide Casino group. At least that's what we were all led to believe. They owned a casino called Sergeant York's in Brighton. Now Jimmy M had more bullshit than a rodeo rancher. In his house he had pictures of himself with numerous celebrities all of which he claimed as personal friends. The trophies, which adorned his fireplace I suspect had been bought by him and engraved as won from race meetings that didn't exist. So I can only tell you of the things that took place when I was in his company.

My first contact with Jimmy was when he asked me to tune and prepare a Super Stock that he had purchased from the winner of that year's British Championship. At the time I was running a motor repair business from a workshop behind my bungalow and to work again on a racing car was great fun. We delivered the Super-Stox to Wimbledon Stadium where Jimmy was waiting with his new top of the range overalls and crash helmet. Complete with silk scarf and racing gloves he drove out to take his place on the front of the grid along side the other novices. As the pace car pulled off cars passed either side of Jimmy until he was near the back of the pack.

Just a few laps later the leaders were starting to lap him, then about half way through the race he pulled onto the centre green and sat on the roof of the car watching to the end. Once the red flag had gone out he jumped into the car and drove it back into the pits. I tried for the rest of the meeting to find the fault that had caused him to pull out but I couldn't find any thing wrong with the car.

A few days later Jimmy telephoned me to tell me he had given the car to a friend and he would in due course collect it from me. I was paid handsomely for my work in cash and with a big tip.

The next time I heard from Jimmy was late one Friday night when he called to ask me if I could collect some motorbikes for him. I'd just built a pickup truck from a Triumph 2000 estate. So off I went to collect two speedway motorcycles. One was a 500 cc bike belonging to the winner of that year's championship *(sound familiar)* and the other was a 250 cc practice bike. Jimmy had booked two places at speedway-riding lessons in Arlington raceway. So off we set.

The lessons started at 10 am on the Saturday morning. Jimmy donned his new leather racing suit and matching crash helmet, whilst I wore my lucky old blue jumper and ripped jeans.

Before you can do any speedway riding you have to get the rear wheel spinning and lay the bike at about seventy degrees to the direction of travel, when going around corners (*a bit like hanging the back out in car racing).* Something Jimmy never quite got the hang of. I'm not saying I was good but I did get round the track at about the same time as the other trainees. By about twelve o'clock Jimmy had fallen off a few times and decided that this sport wasn't for him.

Thrusting a wad of money into my hand he said " See you later ", and drove off in his Rolls Royce. Or at least somebody's Rolls Royce. Later that week their new owner collected the bikes.

The same happened with a Grass Track Side Car Outfit and a Ford Sprint Escort, which ended up in a tree at Goodwood Race Circuit.

My adventures with Jimmy lasted about a year. It was only when he asked me to chauffeur him one night that I realised the world he lived in was in fact a fantasy to most of us. Being in the motor trade I got to drive almost every car available but the offer of driving a Rolls was one I couldn't turn down. Dressed in a second hand dinner suit we set off at about 10 pm for Sergeant York's in Brighton. On arrival I thought I'd have to wait in the car in some other part of the town but once outside the Casino I was told to get out of the car, a doorman got in and drove off to put it in some hidden underground car park.

Jimmy flashed a card to the doorman and we were ushered inside .He went off to the cash desk and came back with a pile of plastic tidily winks. Well that's what they looked like to me. Handing me a pile he said " Go and lose these I'll find you later ". I tried Roulette but with no idea how the game worked my chips just got pulled in by the croupier at the end of each spin. I looked at the craps table but was to shy to queue up to make a fool of myself throwing dice, so I ended up playing cards. As a child my dad played pontoon with me and it looked similar. Sadly it's not and as I sat loosing my chips a scantily clad girl asked me if I wanted a drink.

I politely refused remembering a time in Spain when I had drunkenly entered a brothel and got into a lot of trouble accepting a drink from a scantily clad woman. (*It cost me loss of pride and 3000 pesetas for the antibiotic*).

As I watched the same girl bring drinks for the other punters, I realised that they were free and accepted several glasses of coca cola, which she thought was very amusing.

Once I started to relax I found the restaurant, which served steak dinners at a very cheap price, and after losing my plastic chips sat and ate a steak the size of a dinner plate and watched those playing at the gaming tables. Occasionally I would see Jimmy, gambling at various games and with what looked like serious money. The other players were a curious bunch. One very old lady with diamond rings on every finger seemed to be touching her grandson up as he sat next to her. It was only when she stuck her tongue down his throat that I realised I had seen my first gigolo. Another was a young Arab boy with a gold bracelet that would have dwarfed the one worn by Jimmy Savill .He had two or three blond girls with him all vying to hold on to his arm, as he changed wads of fifty-pound notes for gambling chips. I was later told that it was not uncommon for him to win or lose up to thirty thousand pounds in a night.

(*We paid fourteen thousand nine hundred pounds for our house*).

Hordes of elderly fur clad women played in groups at the roulette table and I was pestered by one of their number who insisted I was Oliver Reed.

It was about 3 am when Jimmy came over to the table where I was sitting. In the dim light the two-inch scar on his right cheek made him look like a gangster.

He told me to collect the car and go home as he had some business to do. I put the small wad of notes he had given me into my pocket and headed for the door. He showed an ID card to the doormen who followed him to the manager's office. As I drove home in the Rolls and parked it in my drive I thought, " I want some more of this ".

Over the next few weeks I drove Jimmy to the Casino a few more times. He told me how he had started as the Managing Directors Chauffer and learned to play all the games, whilst with him in Casinos all over the world. Jimmy had worked his way up, protected by the MD to be the company trouble-shooter.

If a Casino's takings were down Jimmy would go and play the tables until he worked out who was involved with the scam. Apparently it takes at least three people to steal from the company. I was never told much more except that the company never prosecuted anyone.

I once asked Jimmy to put in a good word for me as I'd seen the tips given to the doorman and fancied a job there myself. He told me that as his friend he would never let me work for his employers. He said " once involved you never leave". I think he was exaggerating but one night as he threw several thousand pound onto his living room table he told me that his friend the MD had cancer and things would be bad for him if the man died. A week later that happened and at about 7'Oclock one evening jimmy telephoned and asked me to pick up his Rolls and deliver it along with a brief case to him at an address in Mayfair. This I did and once again accepted a roll of notes and a handshake. As I walked to the tube station I wondered if I would ever see Jimmy again.

Some years later I received a phone call from him during which he said he was running a security dog training school in Spain. My final meeting with him was fifteen years later whilst eating a Curry with some friends in Bognor Regis. A Stocky balding man came over held out his hand and said " Hello Pip how are you It's Jimmy M".

I don't know how much of his story is true but the parts where I was there certainly are. I'm sure he worked for the casino. Cash was in abundance and he was I think respected and feared in his world.

Four or Five years passed. My wife had gone and I continued to run my repair business at home. I gave up Cabaret and started to do children's magic shows so that my daughter could come with me. Some of the other Cabaret acts that I knew worked occasionally as extras or walk-ons in television so I joined several agencies and started to get bit parts on television and in films. Out of the blue Jim the racing driver turned up on my doorstep. He had just purchased a run down racetrack and asked if I would be his commentator.

For some years alongside my other activities I'd been working for the local Hospital radio station with some small success in local BBC radio. So the chance to commentate live on a subject that I had extensive knowledge of was too good to pass up.

The wages weren't great at £50 a day but I was the highest paid on the track as most others did it just for fun. The P.A equipment if you can call it that was of dubious quality and with very little money available from Jim I managed to get it to a standard where the spectators could just about hear what I was saying as the cars roared around the small oval circuit. I even rigged up an old cassette player so I could play music between races.

Spectators for the first few Sunday meetings numbered only a couple of hundred at best. So I spent time with the drivers and got to know their personalities. I'd try to entertain the crowd between races with stories about the drivers. The track and the PA got better and spectators grew to at least five times the number we started with.

I would interview anyone who came near the control box and make up purely fictitious romances and stories about the drivers, mechanics and track staff. The spectators knew every man woman and child who worked on, or around the track through my weekly soap opera, which was The Oval Raceway.

By the end of the second season I was receiving presents from sponsors and food parcels from driver's wives. To this day I get spares from some of the local breakers yards free of charge.

I would stay in my box at the side of the track talking to the crowed from 10 am to after 5 pm without a break, even for the toilet. I did race one more time in a Celebrity race where I came second. Probably my best result ever but not so impressive when you realise we were all driving mark IV Ford Cortina's and the winner's car was only firing on three cylinders. The winner by the way was Jim who passed me on three wheels round the last corner. I'm sure he waited until the end to give the crowd a thrill.

I was approached by other tracks to commentate for them but I was happy in my wooden box at the end of the track feeling that every spectator was a personal friend. Once a year I ran the presentation night at which I sung a few songs, told some jokes, and flirted with loads of women. I was everyone's friend and a safe bet for the women.

My career as a race Commentator ended about two-thirds the way through my third season. My TV work was increasing with better-paid walk on jobs in programmes such as Eastenders and The Generation Game. Some of the days overlapped with my commentating and I am sorry to say Jim saw this as betrayal, so my time with him came to an end.

I see him occasionally and I don't think there are any problems between us. He still runs the track and even though my time there was nearly ten years ago people still stop me occasionally and reminisce on the times they spent listening to me at The Oval Raceway.

So there at the age of about 36 ended my racing days. I never won a race but I won loads of friends. The only groupie I ever had was brought for me and although I lived along side and encountered the aggression .I never became aggressive.

I was there when the sweet smell of Castrol R- 40 filled the stadium, and engines roared free from the restrictions of emission control.

I was there when drivers fought with fists in the pits without the fear of criminal prosecution.

I was there when Racetracks were built in the middle of housing estates and the public watched from their windows without complaining.

I was there when drivers were pulled from their cars injured or dead.

My affair with motor vehicles has so far spanned three decades, and who knows it may reappear in my second or third mid-life crisis. I've never been a winner in either motor sport, or any other activity I've taken part in. But I have taken part, and loved every minute of it.

Dose the fact that I've never won make me a loser? That's for you to decide.

Another School Day

Tired eyes squint to see a half
illuminated bedside clock.
A faint outline shows the small hand,
 pointing towards eight.
Heart Pounding, leaping from the bed,
One leg in trousers, shirt over head.
I Stager to the bathroom,
to splash water on my face.
Time to begin, the get to school race

Pulling back the curtains I call, Time to
get up.
Switch on the iron and pick up a cup.
Skirt and Shirt pressed, bag and shoes
found.
Time for a second call, wakeup, time to
come round.
Sandwiches, crisps, chocolate, biscuit,
and drink.
Yesterdays lunch box is still in the sink.

A quick wipe round and packed for the day.
Come on kid, your breakfast's on its way.
Bread in the toaster, coffee cup in hand.
Wipe off the worktops. Well I'll be damned.

She's huddled on the sofa, duvet wrapped round.
Watching Ninja Turtles, not making a sound.
Get dressed right now, here is your toast.
Do you want tea? You look like a ghost.
Where are my shoes? Go and get your coat.
Turn off the TV. Here's your teachers note.

But Dad its Ninja Turtles. I don't care come on!
But Dad its Ninja Turtles. Its time we were gone!
But Dad its Ninja Turtles. You'll see the back of my hand!
OK Dad but I don't understand?

What don't you understand? Its time we were gone!
That's what I mean Dad The Turtles are still on?
That's a point I think? As I look at the clock.
It's only half past seven. Have I lost the plot?

Sitting next to my baby, the duvet is warm.
We watch Ninja Turtles and time moves on.
Its now eight twenty and we're both late.
Just make it on time to the Primary School gate.
As I watch her go in, Pony- tailed,
Clean pressed, and new.
I stoop to do up the lace on my shoe.

I turn down my collar, and pull up my zip.
I tuck in my shirt, and hook on my belt clip.
What must I look like? The other mums stare.
With their fresh applied makeup
and neatly brushed hair.

I hear mumbled comments. It's ever so
sad.
She's a lovely girl. Lives with her dad.

I head off to work lying under some car.
Ill make the beds lunchtime - prepare
dinner from a jar
More work till three, make a sandwich
for Sam.
Back working to five—then we're off in
the van.
Delivering cars to their owner's homes.
Collecting money and bookings on my
brick mobile phone.

Indoors by six, dinner, shave, and a
bath.
Cousins and Nephews pop in for a laugh.
Seven's kids bath time. On with her
Jammies
Eight o'clock' bed time, after phoning her
nanny.

By ten all is quiet, the kids fast asleep.
I put on the washing that's been left in a
heap.
Plates and cups dried, all put away.
Bed for me now.
Just another school day.

This is a poem from my daughters early school days. I've already told you that there were bleak times and of my insecurity as a parent. But now as I look back, I remember mostly the business of that time.

Always rushing to get to school, or work, or make dinner. I remember the hurt I felt not only for myself, but also for Sam, at the comments and treatment we received from other mothers with children of a similar age.

My main work was mending cars, so my clothes were grubby and ragged. The rheumatism I suffer now comes from the many car gearboxes I changed whilst laying on my snow covered concrete drive, or sitting on hard frozen earth, changing a wheel bearing.

When I stood watching my little girl enter her school. I stood alone. Only a handful out of the hundreds of mothers there ever spoke to me, and then it was only because they were in some way, a distant relative.

I listened to their conversations, which seemed mainly to consist of moans about their husbands, or life in general, and I wondered what their husbands done for a living that could enable them to drive their Suzuki Jeeps and wear the latest designer clothes?

One day Sam asked me if she could bring a friend home for tea. I finished work early on the arranged day, so that I could spend some time with them. Like real mothers do? Sam came home alone looking a little sad. I asked, " Where is your friend?" To which she replied, " Her mum wouldn't let her come. She said our house would be dirty because I don't have a Mum". I can't say any more about that. Even now I have had to stop and take off my glasses and wipe the tears from my eyes. I wonder if that mother knew how much she hurt my daughter and I?

At the time, the man in me had the answer. " Sam you tell her. If my house is dirty. I'll sack the cleaner".
So now let me tell you about the cleaner;
The man in me has sayings that sound so hard and absolute I appear to be chauvinistic and selfish. Perhaps I am, or was. At the time I'm describing I was in my early thirties. I came to the conclusion that (*financially*) Women are best rented by the hour.
Now I know you assume I mean "Hookers", but I don't. I'm thinking of all the times I was told " If you paid me for all the time I spend doing house work and running around after you. I'd be a millionaire". If you've never said it, I know you've thought it.
Well its true. I paid my cleaner £15 a week and she kept my house cleaner than I would ever have kept it. I knew even then that the man in me would forget to change the beds, clean the skirting boards, dust the shelves, and wipe the toilet seat. So I advertised for a cleaner, by putting a card in the local newsagents window. It Read:

Wanted cleaner for light household duties, 4 hours a week.
Must be: Over fifty, Ugly and Married.

Believe it or not I got an enquiry. The lady cheerfully advised me that she fitted the description and asked why those were my requirements. I answered " Well, If you're over fifty and married, you won't be interested in chasing me, and if you're ugly, the many men who come round won't stop you working by talking to you.

She thought my reasoning was sound, and so began a seven or eight year working friendship, which only ended because I moved in with my mother who would clean the house before the cleaner came because she didn't want her to see it dirty. Then, they would sit, drink tea and chat for the two hours that I was paying for a cleaner. In fact my reasoning was faulty, in as far as the lady I employed could talk for England. She often said, " Just tell me to shut up if I go on too much. My husband just walks off when I keep talking". I over came this by giving her a key to the house and being out for the two hours she worked. I came home a few minutes before she left, and just had time for a quick conversation before she dashed off to her next job. She kept my house sparkling clean, Except when I came in with oily boots or greasy hands. But as I used to point out to my wife. I pay the bills and I live here too. (Sorry *man mode again*)
Now I've told you that I bought and sold anything that'd make a profit. So there was always something different stacked up in my garage, drive, house or lawn. I brought three million doorknobs and fixings from a Kitchen manufacturer who was going bankrupt, for two hundred pounds. The volume of these items was about three Ford Transit Vans full. I remember that somehow in amongst that job lot there were, several bull worker exercisers, a couple of bikes and a box of electric wall sockets. These were considered to be, added treasure.
I never gave Sam pocket money. She had the option of several jobs, which would earn her more than enough. They ranged from cutting the grass, to putting six doorknobs in a plastic bag and stapling a card to the top.

Her payment for this was one new penny a bag. On a good evening she could earn a pound. I would then supply the bags on a sale or return basis to car boot people. Who'd sell them for 25p a bag and return me half. That job lot earned me hundreds of pounds over the next few years. It employed Sam, and my whole family had knobs and hinges from that purchase fitted somewhere in their homes. You won't believe it but now some twelve or more years later I still have boxes of knobs and hinges, which I use when building magic illusions or making repairs in my home.

The bulk of the left over stock was sold some years ago to a guy for a hundred quid. He then continued to bag them, and sold the bags mail order through a woodworking magazine. *(I wish I'd thought of that)*. Because I worked most weekends in entertainment, we would plan one-day excursions, and once a month (*usually accompanied by as many kids as we could get in the van, or other family and friends*), we had an adventure. Our outings ranged from a trip to Chessington or Thorpe Park to a day trip to France. The theme parks were great for the kids but caused problems for me. Weighing about twenty stone, I didn't fit in many of the rides. I did go on the Bubble works ride at Chessington, but had to pull the boat along as my weight made it drag on the ground.

Once whilst visiting Chessington World of Adventure with a friend of mine, and her two kids, I had a selfish moment. I decided that I wanted a hot dog, but I didn't want to pay for five. So I sneaked off whilst they went on the Vampire ride.

For three pounds and fifty pence, I purchased the biggest hot-dog I could buy. After pouring a good dollop of sweet American mustard onto it, I took a lustful bite.

As I chewed my mouthful I noticed growing warmth on my pallet. Swallowing hard I realised the American sweet mustard bottle had been filled up with Hot English mustard, and I'd just swallowed a good tablespoon of it.

After throwing the bulk of my hot dog in the bin, I stood in pain filled silence waiting to purchase a can of drink for £1-50.

When I think of that story I remember a girlfriend I had when I was seventeen who used to say, " God pays debts without money". *(O' how right you were Gloria).*

About once every six weeks I'd wake up and decide to go to France for the day. Normally if things weren't going well, or if we'd worked a few weekends on the trot. I'd give Sam the day off school and we'd leave at 6 am to drive to Folkstone, where we'd catch the ferry to Bologne and spend the day wandering around the town. That was it really; we just wandered around looking in the shops. Ending up in La Prisunique. (*A large superstore*). Where we'd buy Chocolate, and Chocolate, and Chocolate,. A little cheese, and some more Chocolate. Then we'd laugh at all the other people who were struggling to carry their duty free beer. Especially when their trolleys, (*which were piled high with crates of lager)*, would bash into something and pierce a can, which then sprayed every one around with a foaming jet of sticky lager.

To save money we'd purchase cold meat and bread for a picnic by the river. My favourite trick when taking new friends, would be to buy some sliced cooked Cheval. Then after we'd consumed our rolls and commented on the lovely lean meat. I'd inform them that they'd just eaten a Horse

To this day if you told my Sam we were going to France, her little face would light up and she'd ask, " Can we get a big jar of drinking Chocolate?"

We never done anything exciting, just wandered about laughed at the other tourists, and ate a horse. Yet those trips seemed a great adventure to us at the time.

My house was continually changing. From the day we bought the two bed roomed bungalow; I would have some DIY project on the go. Before my wife left I had built two extra rooms upstairs. Extended the bathroom and kitchen, and built on a rear sun lounge, which was used as my office. On a scale of one to ten my DIY skills would probably reach four, but with a great deal of help from my friends and relatives, my projects were completed without causing any lasting structural damage to the main building.

One Friday whilst Sam was at school, my nephew Roger and myself decided to renovate the kitchen. By 9-30 am all that was left in the room was two water pipes and a drain. Armed with £150 (*which was my total cash worth*) we set off for the local builders merchants. They looked at us quite strangely when we explained that we didn't really care what make, colour or style the kitchen units were. We just wanted to take them now. "You can't do that" were the salesman's words. Apparently you had to order the units and they came in about six weeks later?

We drove from show room to showroom, until we reached MFI in South Sea. They were putting in a new kitchen display and we were offered one of the kitchens they were taking out.

So at about 2-30pm we arrived home with a vanload of kitchen cabinets and a new sink.

Thinking about it now, Sam didn't bat an eyelid when she walked through the empty room, which that morning had been a kitchen. She just sat quietly in the living room and watched TV. I must have fed her something, but to be honest I don't know what. Her part in this whole story was that she kept out of the way, and went quietly to bed at her normal time. Meanwhile Roger and I set about fitting the new kitchen. I have to admit that it was very much Roger who done the skilled work and I was simply his labourer. By about 10 pm that night we had put together all the base units, and cut the battening to go around the walls. I suggested that this would be a good time to stop, bur Roger wanted to carry on. So we plugged in the hammer drill and began drilling holes in the wall. Once the sink base was fitted, I started to connect the water pipes, and as we worked around the kitchen I put in firstly the fridge, then the freezer. After a bit of plumbing, in went the washing machine and tumble drier. That just left one row of base units and a worktop to go.

Looking at the clock I saw that it was 3-30am. " Shall we stop now Dodge". I asked.

Roger looked up briefly and as the drill started to hammer yet another hole shouted.

" Come on, we've only go a few more holes to drill, let's finish the job".

As he finished drilling the third hole there was a tap on the window. It was my next-door neighbour Paul.

" Are you Ok". He shouted through the glass. I let him in and he explained that his wife had heard the drilling and thought that it was me knocking on the wall, because I needed help.

I put the kettle on and we all stopped for tea. Then Paul joined in and helped us fit the worktop.

I'm not sure what time Les came round but she joined us a while later, being worried about what had happened to Paul.

I fired up the cooker. Sam got up and we all had breakfast. Somehow in les than 24 hours we had striped out the old kitchen, purchased and fitted a new one, and by that afternoon Roger had re-plastered the top half of the walls. That kitchen served us well for the next decade. The story was told at many bar-b-cues and involved me apologising to Les and Paul on a regular basis.

Within the poem that opened this section, there was reference to the friends and relatives who would pop round at all times of the day or night. So I want to explain that my weekdays always started about 7 am and finished about 10 pm, unless I was filming.
In order to try and get some regularity into Sam's life, we had dinner about 6pm. This also happened to be the time that people would come round to pay bills or collect their cars. So inevitably there was always up to six or seven people in our kitchen of an evening.
I never knew how many would be there so I covered every eventuality, by having a freezer full of pre made meals, which I had cooked, and for my little friend Hilary, some Asda ready meals.
The keeping of these came about after one day when I was making Spaghetti Bolognese, our number of three people swelled to ten during the making of the spaghetti.
I waited for the water to boil, and emptied in enough Spaghetti for the three of us.
Hilly had dinner with us most nights, as at the age of about eighteen she decided, " She didn't do cooking".

(*Something that even now at thirty-two has never changed*). So as we sat and chatted a couple of customers arrived. " Something smells nice" they said. " I'm just frying up the mince for the bolognaise, you can have some if you want?"

Now the five of us sat talking, only to be interrupted by a knock on the back door. It was my nephew Gary. " Hi Gaz, want some dinner?" That was a stupid question, as Garry never refuses food. I looked over to Sam. " Nip over the Co-op Sam and get some more mince meat will you please". Sam went off and came back a few minutes later with another pound of mince, which I fried and added to the lot I'd already cooked. As we chatted some other friends arrived who made our number up to something like ten, so I threw some more Spaghetti into the boiling water.

Ten minutes later I served up the Spaghetti Bolognaise and we all sat crunching it, I waited for the first comment. No one said anything, but I realised that the second load of Spaghetti I'd put into the pan wasn't cooked. Believe it or not everyone just carried on eating. One or two said they liked the crunchy bits, Others left them at the side of the plate, but we all had a laugh about it, and enjoyed the gallon of ice cream someone went and got from the co-op.

It occurred to me that I should keep some extra stuff in the freezer, so after that night I always had a few frozen meals for those who came late. Little Sam who was only about eleven or twelve, loved playing the host and handing out dinners and drinks. She knew when her bedtime was and would kiss every one goodnight and just disappear.

I don't know why now at twenty-three she refuses to cook and makes her fiancé get the drinks.

Our local junior school was, and still is considered to be one of the best in the area, and I wanted to get my daughter the best education that I could. There was no way I could pay for private education, so having looked at all of the local schools I managed to get her into a Girls school about six miles away. The deal was that I would have to pay to get her there. So I contacted two local families who were also sending their girls to that school, and we arranged that I would collect and take three others each day, and their mothers between them would get the girls home.

Each morning I would set off at 7.50 am and deliver the girls to school by 8.25.
For the first few weeks I would take them in my Daimler, which looked good but only done about 11 miles to the gallon.
One day I decided to take them in my White Transit Van which was sign written with" Pip Frederick Children's Entertainer". Sam made such a fuss, that I made the vow never to take her in the car again. For the next five years she went to school in the van, or whatever cheap transport I had around at the time. I didn't want my daughter to be a snob. (*I can see her now accusing me of being just that*).
I used to carry a bull horn (*portable amplifier*) in my van, and if it were any of the girl's birthdays, I would sing happy birthday at them as they walked across the car park towards their school. Heads bowed and walking at a trot, they would try to ignore me and pretend I was singing at someone else.
In the eighties that school was so strict that Sam was sent home once because I'd brought a blazer from a non-approved supplier, and sewn on a school badge.

It looked just like all the others but cost thirty pounds less. Even Sam couldn't understand what was wrong with it. But I had to go and buy an approved one so that she could go back. She left that school seven years ago, with a good education and a sense of pride for having attended that place of education.

As I write today, I'm looking at my watch because later this morning I'm going to lecture to a group of year 9 students at that very school. Their dress will vary from part school uniform, to casual clothes, trainers, baseball caps, and piercing, will all be on show.

During my lesson a series of mobile phone tunes will play. The teacher will greet me saying "Hello Mr Frederick, only three months and eight days to go". That's how long he has until he retires.

Everything changes. Some for the good and some for the worse. I've changed so much during my life that I get tired just thinking about the things I've done. Now I'm at what I call my irresponsible age. The pendulum of my life swings from outrageously stupid, to extremely serious. I don't know how long I'll have the energy to continue, but I look back and long for the days when I had to get up at seven, and my life was governed by school times and holidays. When I had to take any job that was offered so that I could pay the bills. Don't get me wrong. I don't want the debt back, but the circumstances of those times made every day different. Adventures just happened, and looking back now there was much fun and laughter in amongst the responsibility.

One thing I have learned is that you can't go back. In the retelling things always seem better or more exciting than they were at the time.

In my life, just like " Forgetting I was married ". It is the man in me that made the mistakes, which give us laughter now. But those same mistakes caused rows and upset which in my case is often forgotten

So now, on responsible days I am serious and efficient, and on other days I am just a boy.

I sometimes go into man-mode and make stupid mistakes, and I dress down to ride my Harley in places where forty –eight year olds would not be expected to go. (*All done within the Law of course).*

To be a man

To be a man is to be afraid.
Afraid to be tender should we be
branded weak.
Afraid to be romantic should we be
emasculated.
Lost then to the support of a soft touch.
A squeeze of the arm for good luck.
Lost then to a gentle kiss for good by.
And the pleasure of receiving a gift of
no practical value.

To be a man is to be afraid.
Afraid to shed a tear should we be
humbled.
Afraid to try should we fail.
Lost then to the release of emotion.
For a story that touches our hidden
heart.
Lost then to the success of a fresh baked
loaf.
Or a risen Yorkshire pudding.

To be a man is to be afraid.
Afraid to ask directions should we be
seen as stupid.
Afraid to speak of problems should we
feel a failure.
Lost then to the support of strangers.
To the chance encounter of a new friend.
Lost then to the council of those who
care for us.
Or the help of those who have empathy
for our situation.

To be a man is to be afraid.
Afraid to play with a child should we be
branded a molester.
Afraid to tell the truth should we admit
fault.
Lost then to the joy and laughter of a
child Splashing in a swimming pool.
Lost then to the forgiveness of confession
Or the release of guilt

To be a man is to be afraid

For many years I was conditioned to believe that to be a man I had to be strong. Accept pain with out flinching. Face my greatest fears without showing emotion. I had to be " The Hunter". Supply the needs of my family without showing the burden. The balance between these responsibilities and honesty of the heart, humbleness and romance has always been hard for me. If as a man I were to touch the arm of a woman, or give her a hug of support. How many I wonder would call me a letch, or see my actions as foreplay to some unwanted forbidden act?
So in an effort to prove myself as" The Hunter" I have undertaken some wild and wacky things.

In the late 70's my hometown of Bognor Regis hosted, "The International Birdman Rally". This event involved jumpers from countries as wide a field as Japan and America. These magnificent men would bring their flying machines and hurl themselves from a tower of scaffolding mounted on the pier. Trying to glide for 100 meters before disappearing under the sea.
In some lame attempt to impress my new wife and kids I entered the competition. At the time there was an advert on television for a dehydrated potato substance called smash. The advert contained two green Martians who would whisk up this powdered potato to a jingle that went something like " Smash makes mash".
First of all I went about building some wings. Dismantling an aluminium table from my dad's old greenhouse. I cut and bolted it together to make a pair of wings about twelve feet across and three feet deep.

I covered them with one of those old candy stripe nylon bed sheets that gave you static when you rolled over. Once assembled I tied two old seat belts from one side to the other. My plan was to simply hold the wings above me and float down. Looking back I can't believe that I really thought I might just float, or that the sheet wouldn't rip. I might have been able to mend cars but my knowledge of aerodynamics was limited to paper planes that dived headlong into the concrete.

My costume was a pair of green tights and an old pair of working boots. A green smock was toped off with a hand painted green scooter crash helmet. Pinned to my chest was a piece of A4 paper with the word "Smash" written on it. I had to borrow a coal lorry from work to get my wings down to the pier. It was probably quite a sight to see a man in green tights driving an eleven tone green lorry with a pair of twelve feet wings tied to the back. Having unloaded my wings in front of the pier and parked my lorry, which took, up seven car spaces. I dragged the whole lot up the pier to sign the disclaimer. I was a bit shocked to be called a comedy entry. I still thought I might have a chance.

Some twenty-five years later I saw a picture of my wife standing next to me in this embarrassingly sad costume and actually felt like going to see her and saying " I am so sorry I put you through that". I thought I was her hero. Here I was about to jump off the pier and risk my life to prove my love for her. In fact I looked so stupid I wouldn't have stood next to me.

The time came and one by one in front of a crowd of over ten thousand *(Including my dad)*.

The Flyers began to throw themselves off the scaffold ramp and plummet into the sea. Some used hang gliders, which managed to fly about thirty metres, but in between the serious attempts, to the delight of the crowd the comedy jumpers would topple off dropping like stones into the rolling waves below. With a war cry, which echoed into oblivion. The man in front of me leapt off the ramp and disappeared from view, clinging madly to the handlebars of his flying bike. Suddenly as I fought to walk up the ramp against the wind, the full realisation of what I was about to do hit me. Here I was a newly married man with three young children. Dressed in a ludicrous costume. About to, (*of my own volition*). Jump 50 metres into the sea, holding about twenty pounds of aluminium and a bed sheet above my head.

In those brief seconds it also occurred to me that the crash helmet and builders boots would not help me float at all. Balanced on the edge of the launch platform I fought bravely to hold my wings parallel so as not to get blown backwards by the wind. *(Which seemed ten times stronger than it was at ground level)*. As I waited for the commentator to tell me it was safe to jump. I looked at the crowd along the seashore. Once again as I so often do in man mode. I felt sick. I wanted to go home. I wanted my mum. I wanted to be anywhere else.

But before the fear took over I was given the all clear and taking a deep breath stepped into nothingness. As soon as my body weight pulled upon the wings they collapsed. Shooting upwards like a pair of clapping hands. My subconscious reaction was to let go of the straps and I never saw my wings again. Without them I was left plummeting seawards.

The normal sensation when in danger of slow motion came into play, and a number of strange thoughts went through my mind as I waited to hit the water. Would my boots be any good afterwards? Why didn't I bring any dry clothes to change into? Would my dad be proud of me?

Suddenly the blue of the sky changed to green. The sharp intake of air my lungs expected as I breathed in was in fact seawater and as I sank further and further under the water every thing became dark. Just as I was about to panic, I was aware of my speed slowing and buoyancy taking over to propel me back towards the surface. At a terminal speed of about 10feet a second my head smashed into the keel of the rescue boat, which had run me over.

Thanks to the scooter helmet my head banged safely along the bottom of the obstacle until I bobbed up on the side. Two large oilskin clad fishermen pulled at my arms as I thrashed with my legs and tumbled into the bottom of the boat, where I rolled around in the entrails of crabs and fish left over from their earlier catch. Eventually I regained my composure and sat on a wooden plank, which was wedged across the boat as they ferried me to shore. Later I sat on the back of my lorry. Wet and smelling of fish guts. Not knowing where my family was and wondering if I had given the key of the lorry to my wife or lost it in the sea. My dad turned up first. " Well done son, " he said. In fact that's all he ever said about that day. He was shortly joined by my wife and kids who were more interested in getting an ice cream than my welfare. Luckily she had the key and produced as women do a towel from somewhere. I really must remind her that I did appreciate her. I just never got around to saying it.

I have got a picture of me on that day and I really must show it to my daughter Sam who was not born until some four or five years later, so that she knows the things I have done with her are not just mid-life crisis, but the things I have always done.

That night the event made international television news. If I am correct the Japanese entry with his hang glider covered the 100 metres and won £1000.
I however wasn't mentioned in either the newsreel or the local paper. My death defying feat went completely unnoticed by all and is not even worth retelling at our family bar-b-cues.
My next story highlights many of the strange and illogical extremes I have gone to in order to head off my inner fears of failure and the outcome, which is often absolute disaster.
I have in fact had four long-term relationships. Each in my perception based on love and a belief at the time in it's lasting for the rest of my life. For various reasons each has ended, but with my never ending optimism I have now learned that what will be will be, and although today I stand alone tomorrow may bring a complete change of heart. The man in me is conditioned that once I connect with a partner, I will do all and everything I can to make them happy and supply the things I deem my responsibility to do. Sadly this perceived responsibility has in the past proven only to make me feel a failure, as often I'm not able to achieve the goals I set myself.

Some years ago I hosted a charity event for a large hotel chain. They were happy with my efforts and offered me a free weekend in any of their hotels.

I was at the time in friendship with a woman whom I had known almost from school. She had two children and was alone with them, and I had Sam.

At that time the fear of failure stopped me from making this a romantic commitment, but I still wanted to do something nice for her.

I chose a very special hotel in Gloucester and with some embarrassment suggested that she and her children might like to accompany us. The first lie came here. So that she would not think I was setting anything up I told her that I had two free rooms and paid for the second myself. She agreed to come and we set about planning a weekend of adventure for the kids.

I meanwhile was driving an old banger, which someone had given me to dump. After a chat with a friend in the motor trade I procured a Daimler with a personal number plate, tax, MOT and two tanks of petrol, for £1000. Which I didn't have but promised to pay off later by fitting clutches to MGB's for him.

Friday afternoon came and we loaded the three kids in the back and regally headed for Gloucester. The man in me felt great and everything was going well, until about twenty miles from the hotel I noticed that every time I decelerated there was a clunk from the rear axel. I dealt with this by slowing down very carefully and accelerating slowly. Our arrival at the hotel was a great relief to me and showing no concern I booked us in and then sneaked off to lie under the car and take note of the two inches of free play in the differential. There was nothing I could do so hoping the car would last the weekend I went inside washed my hands and got ready for the evening meal.

We went down to the restaurant about 7.30pm. Where we decided to order the roast beef for all five of us. After about thirty minutes a young waitress arrived and one by one our plates were placed in front of us. Each was about 10 inches in diameter with two small medallions of beef in the centre, covered by a drizzle of gravy.

To the top right hand side was a budget sized Yorkshire pudding and to the lower left a solitary mange tout. After about another five minutes we were each given a small side plate containing three small boiled new potatoes and two mini corn on the cob. We all looked at the things in front of us and waited for the large tray of vegetables we expected to arrive any time soon.

After about another ten minutes the waitress came over and asked, " Is everything alright sir ". So I explained that we were waiting for our veg. She looked sideways at me and said " Its Nuevo Cuisine Sir". I guessed that meant this was all we were getting. So whist listening to moans from the kids we ate the overpriced mini meal. The lady with me was magnanimous and done everything to reassure me it was not my failure, but after saying goodnight we retired to our separate rooms and I spent the night thinking about the car.

Next morning we all climbed into the Daimler and headed off for Alton Towers theme park. I'd not checked how far it was from Gloucester so two and a half hours and a tank of petrol later we arrived. The clunking had got progressively louder and now it felt like someone was kicking the car every tine we slowed down.

Glad to have arrived I unpacked the food, spare clothes, and video camera borrowed from my brother in law.

Still with a cheerful face I lead our pack round the park and bless her my lovely friend took the kids on all the fearful rides, whilst I used the excuse of filming the event to stay at ground level. Eventually I decided to accompany them on the Thunder river ride. Sitting in the cylindrical boat I held the camera to my eye as we shot through rapids and past obstacles.

I hadn't taken into account that my weight was at least three times that of my companions, and as the boat emerged from a small tunnel, with me in the front. It dug into the water causing a tidal wave to engulf the camera, which let out a loud click and shut off. Once safely off the ride and with water dripping from my clothes. I tried for a few minutes to turn on the camera, without success.

The man in me just wanted to sulk but onward we travelled determined to enjoy the day. At about 6pm we set off for the hotel and apart from the ever-growing clank from the rear axel the journey was uneventful. My companion did mention the noise but seemed to accept my explanation that it was nothing to worry about. By the time we reached the hotel my headache was so bad the clunking of the back axel continued in my skull long after we'd left the car and into my almost sleepless night.

The next morning seemed more hopeful. At least today we were heading home, our plan was to stop at Wooky hole. We made it there ok and apart from a small misunderstanding when I jumped up and down on a metal bridge suspended over an almost bottomless pit. (*Well I didn't know she was afraid of heights and enclosed places*).

We had great fun and I cheered up a bit when I found that the now dried out video camera worked again.

As teatime approached we headed off for the last two hours of our homeward journey. The nearer we got to home, the lighter the weight on my shoulders seemed. With only 30 miles to go I turned off the motorway at Southampton to cruise slowly home on the B roads. Approaching a large junction at Port Solent there was a loud Bang and the car came to an abrupt halt in the middle of a three-lane intersection.

I didn't need to lie under the car to know that the Pinion in the differential had snapped. It had jammed the back axel and so we couldn't even push the car. My companion and the kids were excellent. No panic, no shouting, but inside I felt shit. It took me about five minutes to come up with a plan.

I called my brother in law who came straight out in his escort van. He had AA recovery. So after calling them and being given a two-hour waiting time. I loaded the van with my lady and the kids and drove them home. I returned to the broken down car, which eventually was recovered and delivered, to my front garden where it was dumped unceremoniously at an absurd angle.

None of the negative happenings of the weekend were directly my fault, but the man in me took them as so. I did however learn that one should have some sort of recovery insurance. The friend who sold me the car supplied a second-hand rear axel and after a day lying in the mud fitting it. I was back on the road. Happily planning our next trip, which ended up with the rear brake pads wearing out and me driving around Devon with a pair of mole grips clamping off the rear brake pipe.

So being afraid is an inherent part of me as a man. I don't know how many of my gender will admit to the same but I'm sure they all have that fear somewhere inside.

I have to say that in some cases the ladies I have been with made no negative comment when disaster hit, and it was only the perception of failure that made me succumb to my inner fears.

Having learned at a somewhat late age that there is nothing wrong with being afraid, I deal with it now by not being afraid to be afraid.

Looking back at the many mishaps and unforeseen problems I've encountered, when trying to do the right thing, they now become adventures and stories to be re told with laughter.

My last short story will I hope show you how a single word or sentence can destroy a man's self-confidence. I met a lady through my daughter who was going through a very lonely time. Her life had turned upside down and she was having real problems with transport. I decided that I should help her just to show that sometimes a stranger will care, simply because someone should.

I called in a favour and obtained a very cheap car. After servicing and making it as safe as possible. I polished the fading paintwork, and at the arranged time I arrived with the car at a local pub. The sparkle in the woman's eye made me feel that I had at last achieved something good. Until standing by the driver's door she said. " It doesn't have a radio".

I felt as if my heart had been torn from my chest and squeezed until every drop of blood dripped onto the gravel floor.

How was she to know I had driven 20 miles to collect a radio, which didn't work and then brought two more in a boot sale, which also didn't work. I know she didn't say those words with malice or bad thought. It may even have been a joke. But never the less the man in me felt that he had failed again.

A recent happening has however given me hope that the man in me may be learning still..
Just as I had come to believe that whatever we men do for a lady it would more often than not be less than perfect. I did buy two separate things for a lady I know, and they turned out to be the right thing. She was very happy with her gifts and made no criticism or negative comment. That gives me hope. So maybe the fear of failure made me do better once I realised it was there.

Packing for my holiday

My suitcase lays empty on the bed.
Ready to receive a vacations wardrobe.

Seven nights, Seven pairs of socks.
Seven boxers, Seven T shirts.
One best trousers, one pair of shoes.
One pressed shirt, one Motorcycle News.
I don't need to pack any more,
I always take too much,
but now I'm not sure?
Perhaps just a blazer for the evening
chill.

A tie, some cufflinks, and a few
headache pills.
Swimming shorts, a paperback book,
Trainers for that casual look.
Safety pins, glue, torch, batteries, and
spares.
Won't take too much.
I can buy more stuff there.

Perhaps just one hat, spare sunglasses
and Some gel for my hair.
A beach towel, some tissues,
my pajamas, and teddy bear.

Don't need any more,
when I'm there I'll buy loads.
I can just squeeze a bit more,
in between my clothes.
A couple of pot noodles, some tea bags
and a spoon. Some wet wipes,
suntan lotion, diahroea pills,
And a spare mobile phone.
Don't need anything else,
I can buy more on site.

Just my travel clock, waterproof coat,
And cream for insect bites.
Better take my CD, and a few discs to
play.
Might need my palm top TV for a rainy
day.
Some plasters, a pen, my toothbrush and
comb.

A sewing kit, razor, and shaving foam.
Don't need anything else.
I'ts only a week after all.
Just a flask, my table tennis bat,
and blow up stress ball.

Lid down, Zip fastened,
Straps wrapped around.
Placed by the door
for when I come down.

Passport in pocket,
tickets In hand.
I board my plane
For a far off land.
As I fasten my seat belt
And head for places unknown.

I think SHIT.

I've left my suitcase by the front door at
home!

There's no deep and meaningful stuff in that poem. I wrote it this morning whilst I was having a coffee in the gym.

I wanted to tell you about some of the funny things that have happened whilst I was on holiday, and as I'm about to go to Egypt with my daughter and her fiancé, packing seemed to be a good topic.

Until I was in my late twenties the furthest I'd been was the Isle of White. My first taste of foreign travel came during a particularly bad time in my marriage. I'd obtained my first credit card and I was so pissed off, I walked into a travel agent and said, " Where's the cheapest place I can go today?" Half an hour later I left with a ticket in my hand for a coach leaving Kings Cross later that day. Lorette De Mar was my destination. Two weeks bed and breakfast including return coach travel cost me £78.

The prospect of twenty four hours on a coach didn't seem too daunting, and having thrown every item of clothing I owned into the biggest suitcase I could buy I caught the train to Victoria and dragged my luggage across London on the underground.

Luckily I had a passport because sometime before I'd gone on a day trip to France with my family. Having had a blazing row with my wife on the way to the ferry, I spent most of the day thinking about how no one checked who we were when we boarded, so if I threw her overboard, I could deny ever being there. I didn't do it, just worked out how I could.

With my case safely loaded I found my place on the coach. It was only about two thirds full, and as so often happens, no one sat next to me.

As we trundled along I listened to the other passengers conversations and quickly worked out the various personalities.

The lady behind me was showing everyone a photo of her famous cousin. Someone called Millicent Martin. Apparently she was a variety song and dance lady. Believe it or not some ten years later I worked with the same Ms Martin on a TV series called Moon and Son, I didn't tell her that I'd once met her cousin. Anyway I was quite impressed with the bus, it had coffee making facilities, and a toilet. Sadly I didn't fit in it, but the bus stopped about every three hours so I managed to pass water in three different countries within the same day. (*Definitely something to tell your mates about. It's a man thing*).

Eventually we arrived at our destination and along with another couple I was dropped at the door of a small family run hotel in the center of town.

Inside were gathered about twenty people waiting for the Panorama rep. When she arrived we were given a welcome speech and a glass of champagne. I don't like speeches or champagne so I left my case by the door and went off to look around. I was joined by a welsh man called Richard, who insisted that we stop at every bar and have a cuba libra ,
(*Rum & coke*).

By about seven o'clock that night we were both completely lost and in no state to try and find our way. We found ourselves in a very small and dimly lit bar in what one could only describe as the bad part of town. Women of all ages and sizes kept asking us to buy them drinks, and Richard who had very little tact, told them to "piss off".

Finally after the particularly loud rebuff of one large elderly lady.

A big hairy Spaniard came over, punched Rick on the nose and threw us both out. As we sat in the gutter outside the bar telling our story to a couple of passing English lager louts. They asked " Why did you go into a brothel if you didn't want a woman?" Seems like a good question.

Lunchtime the next day we bumped into the panorama rep, who told us that if we didn't book in by 2 o'clock they would give our rooms to someone else. As I was handing over my passport to the hotel owner I met Richards girlfriend. She didn't say much to me because she was too busy slapping Richard on the back of the head as she kicked him up the stairs.

The next morning as I sat trying to work out if my glass of orange and flaky bun thing was in fact a continental breakfast, or whether eggs and bacon would follow it, Richard's girlfriend came and sat opposite me. She turned out to be a really nice woman. Apparently Rick had food poisoning. I don't know how. He hadn't eaten anything since I met him. I think it was alcohol poisoning. Well he didn't come down for the rest of the week. Sandra that was her name told me that in Wales there are seven women for every bloke, and that she was lucky to have one even if he was a piss head.

So for the rest of the holiday, each evening Sandra would come clubbing with me and we'd arrive back at the hotel in the early hours of the morning to strange looks from the owner. One morning at breakfast he asked me what my relationship with her was. I explained the best I could but I don't think he understood, because every time he saw us together he would wink at me and stick up his thumb.

During the day I was left to my own devices as Sandra went shopping or sun bathing.

I enjoyed sitting with a bottle of San Miguel and watching the cars being towed away. Or the traffic wardens spinning their chromium plated guns.

One day I fell asleep leaning against a pile of deck chairs. My black beret hat had fallen off of my head, and as I woke up I could see it by my side full up with hundred peseta coins. As I came to I could see the deck chair attendant coming down the beach asking people for their money. They were pointing at me. I picked up the hat and walked quickly away. Later I had a count up and had earned two thousand pesetas whilst I was asleep.

About four days into the holiday, I was walking along the promenade when one of the flat cap brigade from my coach came running up to me and thrust a business card into my hand saying. " It's been days since we had any proper food. We've just found this place and they do a proper roast dinner, with Yorkshires and everything". He then ran off handing out the cards to other English tourists, I couldn't help thinking, " Why would you come to Spain and look for an English roast dinner?"

Even though I was a virgin traveller, I decided to jump on a bus and have a look round Barcelona. It struck me that it was just like London; it even had a Mac Donald's. I stopped to watch a bull fight and fight off the hookers. Then I noticed a member of the Guardia and decided to get a picture of me standing next to him. I found another tourist and asked him to take the photo. As I joined the policeman by his car, I placed a friendly arm on his shoulder.

Next thing I knew, my hands were behind my back in handcuffs.

The tourist threw the camera at me and ran off as I was bundled into the car and driven to the police station. I wasn't treated roughly, but I have to admit to being a bit scared. Well actually I was crapping myself.

After about an hour a policeman who spoke English came into the room. He explained that the other Policeman hadn't wanted his photo taken, as he was unshaven. He could have explained that to me couldn't he? Surely arresting me was a bit of an over reaction. Anyway after apologizing and offering to give him the film (*which he didn't want*) I was released and after a hours ride on public transport arrived back at Lorette De Mar.

The next day I decided to do some shopping. I brought loads of clothes and a couple of leather jackets. Armed with my new credit card my last stop was the jewellers, where I purchased a gold watch (*well it wasn't real gold, just gold colored*) for three thousand pesetas. That afternoon I sat on my hotel bed admiring it, when I noticed that my new watch didn't have a second hand. I held it to my ear and could hear nothing. Bastards I thought. I've been ripped off.

I stomped back to the shop, throwing open the door and thrusting the watch at the man behind the counter saying " No magusta ". I think that means no good? He looked at the watch and tried to hand it back. " No magusta, No magusta". I said in a raised voice. His English was as bad as my Spanish, but eventually I got the message that I was to come back in an hour.

I spent that hour getting ready for a big argument if I didn't get a working watch there would be trouble. I wasn't going to be a mug punter.

One hour later I walked into the shop, face as black as thunder, and raised to my full height. There behind the counter was a pretty young woman, who spoke perfect English." I've come to collect my watch; it's a gold one. I brought it this morning and it doesn't work". The girl reached beneath the counter and handed me my watch saying.

" We can't find anything wrong with it". Putting it to my ear I said " Its not ticking". The girl smiled at me and said, " It's a battery watch".

I probably didn't grovel quite as much as I would have if it happened today, but I was humbled.

My final purchase was mad with the encouragement of my new friend Sandra. I stopped outside a shop to admire an almost life sized toy donkey. " You must buy that for your little girl" she said. So I did.

Everything was great until I left the coach at King's Cross and had to try to drag my suitcase with one hand and carry a four foot donkey in the other. I got many strange looks as I traveled across London, on the underground, and I thought that I might be charged for an extra ticket on the main line.

Eventually I got home and next time I saw Sam I gave her the giant donkey. With a gleeful smile she jumped on it, and the legs collapsed.

My credit card now had twelve hundred pounds owing. So this was not a good time in my life. Later on when I had sorted my domestic problems. I didn't want to pay it. So over the next few years I made small payments to the bailiff, and eventually with six hundred pounds still owed Barclaycard decided not to chase me any more.

Some seven or eight years later however, they forgave me, and I now owe them thousands again. The only difference now is that I am having fun spending their money, so I do pay it back (*most of the time*).

That was my first experience of international travel, and even though it was at the budget end, I learned that if you don't take it too seriously and you buy late, you can get some really great deals.

A few years later after my divorce, I took a mortgage to pay out my wife, and added just enough to take Sam to Disneyland Florida. It may seem that I am irresponsible, but that is only when I am on my own. Our Florida trip was a reward for my little girl, after all the upset and stress she had gone through. So I paid top dollar and we had the best holiday of our lives.

There are two short stories I want to tell you. The first re enforces my belief in Random acts of kindness.

On the morning after our arrival, I was sitting outside the hotel on International Drive, when I saw an old couple struggling with their cases. I went over and helped them get to the taxi. The old man offered me some Disney tickets, which I refused. He persevered until I took them. When the couple had gone I looked at the tickets, which had four days each, left on them. They saved us over two hundred pounds.

Random acts of kindness will feature I am sure in later stories, but for now I will only say. It is my belief that they start the ripples of good fortune, which will (*when you least expect it*) bring kindness back to you.

We took one day out from visiting the many wonderful and exciting things in Florida, and whilst we sat by the pool a man came over and started chatting. " I know you from somewhere" he said. As modestly as I could, I answered " You've probably seen me on TV". "What have you been in?" he asked. " Eastenders" I answered "No"- " The Bill?" " No"- " Generation game?" –"No". " French and Saunders?" " No". Sam joined in " Boon? "- "No"- " Casualty?"- "No" – " Hannay?"- "No".

"I know what you've seen me in. I did a series of adverts for Thomas's Old English Muffins. It's shown all over America". The man looked at me hard and said " No I saw you in the Bird in hand Pub near Chichester , you were dressed as a pirate".

For ten years after that, foreign travel was too expensive for us so we went camping in the New Forest. Along with my nephew Roger and his family we would arrive on a Friday night and light up the bar-b-cue, which would burn until we went home on Sunday afternoon. Packed in my white transit van with the words Pip Frederick Children's Entertainer painted on it. We had everything you could need. Tables, chairs, water bombs, super-Soakers, bikes, and any other toys we could carry. Every Kid, Mum Dad and Grandparent was welcome to join in, as we chased around soaking each other and throwing burgers at any one who wanted one. When the ice cream van came round, dodge and I would take turns in giving him £20 and saying. " Give the kids ice cream till the money runs out". (*Try it sometime. It's worth it just to see the salesman's face*).

Those were the days when people weren't afraid to play with kids. When a stranger would help a child without fear of accusations, and before you had to do a risk assessment to play with a water pistol.
One night whilst about ten of us were sitting round the bar-b, a couple arrived and pitched their tent. We gave them a burger and a bottle of beer, and they told us they were newly weds.
They excused themselves early and retired to bed. I don't think they knew much about camping, because as we sat watching, they turned on their battery light and proceeded to have sex (*in some interesting & educational positions*).
Silhouetted against the canvas they made a marvellous show, and as they finished our group (*which had grown considerably*), gave them a round of applause and a cheer. The light went out and they were gone when we woke up the next day.
We never quite found the right way to explain to the kids. Why some donkeys have five legs? But we made loads of new friends and soaked hundreds of kids with the biggest super-soakers we could buy. (*What's the point of being grown up if you can't have the best toys?*)
Apart from some day trips to France, which will have to wait for the next book, our travelling was to my perception fairly normal and comparatively un-eventful until my fortieth birthday, when my old friend Daff bought a two-day coach trip to Paris for us to go on.

I know she won't mind me telling you, but after her breakup with my old boating pall Roger.

She lived on a very low income; in fact so low that she would buy all the left over vegetables from the greengrocer at the local market, and piled high by her back door, they became her main food source. In fact that's probably why she's a vegetarian.

Well most of the time, except when she comes to my Mum's, when she eats lamb. Don't ask me why?

Any way, off we went at 6-30 am from Havant bus station. I had my bag packed with far too much stuff as usual and Daff had a hold all and two plastic carrier bags, both of which she carried onto the bus.

Carefully she put one in the rack over the seat, and the other down by her feet. Luckily Daff has always been very slim, in fact when she was younger she was a dead ringer for Olive Oil, you know Popeye's girlfriend. Well thanks to her slimness, I managed to wedge myself into the seat next to her.

As we traveled towards Dover, out from the plastic bag she pulled a crossword book and by the time we got to the ferry, all of those around us were joining in with our puzzles.

Mid afternoon saw our arrival at the Hotel in Paris. The Coach driver told us that although there was no official dinner that night, he was going to a place on the Moulin Rouge, Where for £10 each you could eat and drink as much as you wanted. Sounded good to me so I brought two tickets.

Before dinner we went on a boat trip along the river Seine. That was when we first had to try and explain out relationship to the other travellers. It seems the phrase " Were just friends" is always greeted by a wink and a smile? It was about this time that Daff awoke from a daydream with the words " Damn I forgot to put the chicken in the bath ".

I knew her well enough not to ask her to expand on that statement, and we went on to have a great evening. I had two steaks and she had two bottles of wine, well three or four if I remember correctly, and I do because I was drinking diet coke. In the morning Daff got up first. As I waited for her to finish in the bathroom, I had a look at the tour brochure, which said we were going to the Eiffel tower. Daff emerged from the bathroom and I entered. Pulling back the shower curtain where I was greeted by a Tesco's carrier bag, sitting in the middle of the bath. " Daff. What's in the carrier bag ? " I asked. " That's the chicken" she replied, as if it was the most normal thing in the world. I decided to just wash myself, and my hair in the sink, and after getting dressed, I had to research the chicken a bit further.

" Daff , why have we got a cooked chicken in the bath?" She then opened her hold all and pulled out a couple of pot noodles, saying. " I thought you might get hungry so I cooked a chicken and I brought these pot noodles to save money". Today I would say Bless her, but then I just thought Silly Cow".

I decided we should leave the chicken in the bath. I thought it might be funny when the cleaner came in, and after our continental breakfast *(which explains why French women are so thin)* we joined the Coach to go and see the tower.

Unfortunately it was a foggy day, so Daff decided that it didn't look far to the Louvre and we should go and take a look at the Mona Lisa. After arranging to meet the coach in three hours time we set off along the riverbank. " It must be just up ahead," she said, looking at her tourist map. Fifteen minutes later, sounding like one of her kids I asked " How much further Daff ?"

" Not much it should be just up ahead ". It probably wasn't as far as I remember but after what seemed like a ten-day hike we arrived at a glass pyramid in the middle of the square. We could see people inside but couldn't find the entrance.

Eventually we found it in a completely different road about a quarter of a mile away. Once checked for explosives and weapons we were allowed inside. Daff thought the handheld metal detector batons were funny. *It reminded us of a vibrator I gave her for Christmas some years earlier. Its ok I gave every woman I knew one that year. You see my cousin Steve brought a load from a man who brought them off a salvage company who reclaimed them after they sank in a cargo ship in the China Sea. I paid him twenty-five pence each. You had to give them a thump to start the motor going and they were a bit noisy. But I'm sure they still achieved their purpose, which we all know is to emasculate men. Isn't it?*

Once inside the museum we proceeded to explore a labyrinth of rooms and corridors, at the end of which an arrow directed us towards "The Mona Lisa". Being a man I would have been happy to just browse the items on show, but Daff had to read every note, and the history of each individual artifact. Having read all there was to digest in the Egyptian mummy display, the last notice said. "These artifacts are replicas of the originals which are kept in Luxor Museum." Or something like that. I'd spent an hour looking at a load of plastic fakes!

We trundled on for another hour looking at historical items and following the signs, which continued to point to "The Mona Lisa".

Then as we followed the crowd it disgorged into a large room, which was full of people from all walks of life. At the far end was a lit display containing a painting, which was about eighteen inches wide by two feet tall.

Was that it?

It looks more like the Mini Lisa.

As I stood squinting to see if the eyes really followed you. The flashing camera bulbs seemed like strobes. It is true the Japanese tourists had two or three different cameras hanging around their necks. I couldn't be bothered to fight my way to the front. I'd seen the painting that was good enough for me.

Back at the Hotel, we ate the pot noodles and collected the chicken from the bath as we made our way to the Coach for the return journey. It was with some sadness that I watched Daff hand over our little traveling companion to two truckers we met on the ferry. They carelessly ripped off her legs and devoured the most traveled foul in Europe before our very eyes. Reducing out menage a' trois to two. My birthday is in December and it was between minus 8 and minus 11 degrees over that weekend.

So we both came home with colds, but it was a great birthday present thanks Daff.

(*Perhaps not for the chicken*).

It's probably the case that my holidays are no more exciting or problematic than any one else's. It could even be that I put myself in stupid situations, but I could tell you several stories about every single trip I've been on. Like the puncture we had in the coach, which left us, stranded about 500 yards from the ferry, and (*for health and safety reasons*) we were not allowed to walk to it.

Or the time the coach was late and we were sent home in a taxi from Maidstone, and my mum made the driver stop and have dinner at midnight. Or the time Daff got high just by wandering past the Brown Café's in Amsterdam. Or the time we took a wrong turning and had to climb Cologne cathedral. But they are minor incidents compared to our Coach trip to Italy.

For two reasons we went mainly on what I would call the blue and white stripe holidays.

These were the cheapest possible ways of seeing Europe. I'm afraid I do like a good deal, and a seven-day coach trip to Italy, including bed, breakfast and several sight seeing trips, for £135-00. Looked like the deal of the century.

Daff always struggled for money, and insisted on paying her half of everything (Bless her).

So with Sam grown up and at college. We set off for an extremely odd adventure.

Our day started at 5-30 am. As we stood in the wooden shelter at Bognor coach park.

I mentioned to Daff that I had never seen any coaches from our tour company picking up there. We stood completely alone as the wind blew leaves across the tarmac, which reminded me of tumbleweed drifting across some deserted western town.

Just as I was thinking we'd been conned, a blue and white mini bus pulled in. " Are you for the Italy trip" the driver asked. As we were the only people there I guess we were. Our luggage was thrown in the back and off we went. My heart sank with the thought of travelling for a week on a fifteen-seater transit, but as we trundled along the driver explained.

" I take you as far as Brighton bus station, where you pick up a coach which will take you to Dover".

An hour and a half later after stopping at Littlehampton, Worthing, and Hove, to pick up other passengers, we were left standing with our luggage outside Brighton bus station.

During the ten minutes we waited for our connection, some of the other travelers told us that they'd come from Darby, and had traveled overnight changing buses twice already.

Our bigger bus arrived and we then set off for Dover, stopping at regular intervals to collect new passengers. By the time we arrived at the ferry port, we'd been on the road for Six hours, to cover a distance that I could have driven by car in about two. There in the Coach park was a line of blue and white coaches numbered from one to thirty five.

Our driver read out a list of numbers and corresponding destinations as he threw our cases onto the tarmac. Our group dispersed and wandered around like headless chickens until each found the tour bus for their holiday. " No time to go in the café, we can eat on the ferry " the new coach driver said. So we travelled the two hundred yards to the boat, and once aboard left the bus to enjoy our channel crossing. In fact it was enjoyable. Having left home some eight hours before I was starving, and made Daff come and have a cooked breakfast.

We knew the journey was going to take 36 hours, so as usual Daff had her carrier bags packed with, sandwiches, water, boiled eggs, crossword books, and stuff which might come in handy as we sat in our sardine seats for the next day and a half.

During the first few hours of travel through France we stopped once at a service station.

Unfortunately the toilets were broken, so being one of the main stopping points for coaches they had imported twenty-three portable fiberglass toilet cubicles, which stood unceremoniously in the car park. I took a video of Daff cueing up to use one, and then after looking in the door deciding that she didn't want to go that much. I really wanted to stand in the middle of the car park and shout " we know what your doing" but Daff wouldn't let me.

After spending twenty Francs on a cup of coffee, we boarded the coach for the next leg of our journey.

The bus did have a toilet but apart from the fact that I didn't fit in it. There were two large illuminated figures in the panel above the driver's head. One lit up green, when the toilet was vacant, and then when someone went in, the red one would light up.

This seemed to me to be a waste of time, as anyone who stood up was obviously going to the toilet. There was nowhere else to go. You couldn't even jump off without the driver opening the door. So it was pretty obvious when the toilet was in use.

The coach also had tea-making facilities, and for fifty English pence, one of the two drivers would make you a cup of tea or coffee. Unfortunately this broke about two hours into our trip. At about the same time as the toilet got full up.

For the rest of the outgoing time we were entertained by the jovial banter of the two drivers, who took turns in sleeping in a little cupboard under our seats.

The usual mix of personalities exposed themselves, and we completed two crossword books with the help of the other passengers.

For some reason about twenty-four hours into our journey, at about 5 am someone decided to start a sing along because they didn't like what was on the radio. After about two minutes of " It's a long way to tiparary". The two singers gave up, and we obtained a few hours of broken sleep.

I think that on this journey I was not as engaging as I could have been, and Daff was left to read for much of the time. At the age of forty-one, as my little friend Hilary would say." I was loved up ". I'd met a woman, who was unlike any I had known before. She walked straight into my heart, and occupied my thoughts completely. At the time I thought that I was in control of my emotions, and had certainly put my heart away. But now as we travelled further away from her, the emptiness in my chest became almost unbearable. Even now as I think of that time, the shadow of that feeling is still there.

I remember little of our arrival at the Hotel as my only concern was to get my mobile phone working so that I could for a few minutes speak to the woman I was missing so deeply.

Daff went off to the bar, and I stood outside on the steps in the rain trying to work out where you put the + on the number or if I should add 44. Eventually after spending the first two hours of my time in Italy, standing in the rain, I got through, and spent ten minutes speaking with my new love. Now I was ready to continue with my holiday.

Once installed in our room, I unpacked my case, which as usual contained much more than I would need, but still not enough. I thought I'd been good in packing twelve pot noodles of varying flavors.

Looking round the room I asked, " Have you seen the kettle ?"

We both hunted all around but couldn't find it. Daff went down to reception and asked, but was told there are no kettles in the rooms.

Whilst she was doing that, I looked a little closer at our de-hydrated meals. I must have been in man mode when I brought them, having not looked closely at the time of purchase. I'd picked up Pot Mash. (*This was a trial product, which didn't take off*).

As I sat with my stomach rumbling I went into man-mode. Disappearing into the bathroom I shouted back "Don't worry Daff, I'll use the hot water from the shower".

After running the shower for several minutes, it was little more than warm, but in my desperation I placed the pot mash about three inches below the showerhead. The force of the water blew the powdery mash out of the container and all over my hair. Fully clothed, I staggered about in the shower trying to switch it off and ended up wearing most of the mushy cold dinner.

As in previous tales, I didn't give up and eventually managed to get a mixture, which resembled something, that had already been eaten by someone before. It was cold, and even in my state of hunger indigestible. So we decided to walk to the supermarket and do some shopping.

The shop we found resembled my local co-op. Being a tad bilingual Daff went off to make sure that they would accept my credit cards. We had about a hundred quid in lira, and another hundred in sterling, but armed with my new credit cards, *(which had adverts assuring us they were accepted in 100's of countries)*. I decided to use them instead of cash.

I had absolutely no knowledge of Italian, and trusted Daff to know the few words necessary to get us through, as she seems to have a natural ability for languages. On her return she told me that the manager had assured her that they took all types of credit cards. We decided that she should buy all her presents now so that they were paid for on my card and we could use our cash for odds and ends during the week.

So off we went on our trolley dash. Two bottles of Brandy for Gemma, (*that's her daughter*), cigarettes, cigars, some beer, dates, (*why do people buy them?),* soft drinks, crisps, nibbles, loads of other non descript things, and a jar of pickled stuff, the exact contents of which I never discovered.

With our trolley piled high we made our way to the checkout, where a nice little girl proceeded to check every item and with a rasp of the till our bill was totalled. Not even trying to understand Italian numeracy, I handed over my clean new Barclay Card. The girl looked at it and with a shake of the head, handed it back to me. Ok lets try my unused Master Card?

With another shake of the head that card was returned. Alliance and Leicester- Bank of Scotland- Beneficial bank, and Sainsbury's, all failed the test. Daff looked around for the manager, ready to give him a roasting, but he'd gone home.

The queue now forming behind us was getting loud and their ambiance seemed more threatening than the usual waving of arms used in Italian conversation. So I got out my wallet and handed over the entire contents in lira. Then made Daff hand over hers.

The cashier counted out the amount she wanted and the wad of notes we had left looked big, but amounted to about fifty pence.

That was all the cash we had for the week, but never mind we had the credit cards and surely someone must accept them?

Back in the room we unpacked our goods, and decided to try some of the pickled stuff from our jar. I think it was some sort of fruit, but the green mould, which covered the outer skin, put me off and the revolting taste (*not unlike cold parsnips*) made me leave the opened jar on the sink.

Obviously the man in me has to blame Daff for buying it, however neither of us ate any more and the jar was left in the bin on our departure. So that nights dinner consisted of a warm pot mash, some crisps, a cake, and a mouldy pickled thing.

Over the next day or two we tried several restaurants and found that in the places we were visiting Visa and MasterCard were unheard of. I'm not sure how but we did manage to get some money, I think I spent some time in a bank one afternoon and got cash on one of the cards. Whatever I got, I remember that we still had to be careful what we spent.

Luckily the outings we went on were included in the price of the holiday so we only needed cash for food and gifts.

I have to say that one of the great things about traveling with Daff is that she is so laid back. (*Unless we get ripped off, then she's a rotweiler*). One of our trips took us to Vatican City. Now I will probably get an ear bashing for saying this, but Daff is a staunch Roman Catholic (*when it suits her*). I think her religion is a bit like her vegetarianism.

Most of the time she conforms, but sometimes (*like me with marriage*), She forgets.

Well of course we had to visit the Vatican. We paid our seven pounds each and began a trek through halls and vaults, which made the Louvre in Paris look like a cupboard. Every artifact and painting was priceless and as usual for the first couple of hours we had to read every explanation of the history of each item, whilst following the signs pointing to " The Sistine Chapel,

(*is that how you spell it?).*

At the risk of heresy, I started to question why with all this wealth, the Vatican hadn't sold some and sent food to feed the third word, or some other act of humane kindness to the bulk of mankind?

By now I was bored and tired, but Daff was so inspired by the things we were seeing, that I continued uncomplaining just to see the wonderment on her face. At one point we entered a room with the biggest paintings I have ever seen. If I said they were as big as the side of my house I wouldn't be exaggerating. Daff explained to me their religious meaning, and that in one particular picture there was semi hidden the claws of the devil. I have to say I was impressed by the brightness and clarity of the colours, and on spotting one of the claws, I reached across the thin wire, which made us stand about two feet from where the picture hung, and put my finger on the painting calling " Hey Daff look there's one". Before the words had left my mouth, the sound of an alarm hit my ears, followed by a uniformed man who said something in Italian that needed no translation. The waving of his arms and his facial expression told me " Don't touch the painting you prat ".

173

Sheepishly I made apologetic gestures and moved quickly towards Daff, who was laughing, but I know secretly she was thinking I was an idiot.

Finally just as with the Mona Lisa, our group disgorged into the Cysteen Chapel, I suppose I should have realized it would be small, simply because it is a chapel. But somehow the photos I'd seen made it seem much bigger. So once again to me size does matter, and I was disappointed (*it's normally the woman who says that isn't I?. Sorry man-mode again*). I stood feeling like a sardine alongside hundreds of others, holding my head back to it's full extent in order to see the paintings which we had all travelled so far to gaze upon. That took me about ten seconds, then whilst Daff looked lovingly heavenwards, I watched as people fell over the idiots who were laying down in order to get a better view. That was much more entertaining.

Having spent three hours walking around the Vatican, with Daff suffering my skeptical comments, we came out to have a look at the Vatican City. On our way in I'd seen a man putting out hundreds of stacking chairs, they were now full of nuns. A man dressed in white came onto a balcony, waved, and went back inside. The nuns let out a sigh of excitement, got up and left. The little man came back, and put the chairs away.

A couple of interesting points about Vatican City: You can post a letter or card from there and get a special stamp. (*Which costs 30% more than a normal one*). You can buy a cup of coffee there, (*it costs £5*). You can buy loads of plastic memorabilia, (*why?*)

You may think I'm a bit hard on God and his followers. Actually I'm not. I once visited East Germany; a few weeks after the great wall came down. Each day a local government official escorted me to churches and places of historical value. One day he asked me what religion I was, so I told him." I don't follow one religion. I try to perform one act of random kindness each day, and help those who will never know that I have done it .I believe that if we all care for the welfare of our fellow men, and we work towards passing to a better place. Then we all believe in the same thing". His answer was
" No that can't be possible, because our god is better".
Suddenly I understood why people fight and argue over religion, and I don't want to be part of that conflict.

So as my God always does, he paid me back for my heresy with a vengeance.
We decided to have a walk around Rome. Daff as usual was miles ahead, looking at some monument or in a shop window. I meanwhile was walking calmly along the pavement of a narrow street, when a Renault 5 for no reason at all, swerved off of the road, mounted the pavement, knocked me into a wall, and drove off.
I wasn't too hurt and my camera was ok, so dusting myself off I smiled and thought again of the words " God pays debts without money".

We visited loads of other places, where we had no trouble, but because of that fact I don't need to write about them. I made it through the week, calling my new love each night at six o'clock and telling her of the day's adventure and as the week came to an end my feelings were mixed, part of me wanted to continue travelling and part of me desperately wanted to come home to my lady. I didn't think until now how hard it must have been for her, knowing that I was away, staying in a room with another woman. The day before we left to come home, we finally found a restaurant in Pompeii that would take Visa, so we pigged out on pizza.

That evening someone told us that there was a water supply just up the hill, which had healing powers, Daff decided she needed a bottle of it. So off we went, you have to remember we are in the middle of a small town. It doesn't look to me, anything like a place of miracles.

The hill went up at a very steep angle, and as usual tour destination was not " just up the hill". It was up the hill, and up a bit further, and then just up a bit more. Finally we arrived. I knew we had arrived, because there in the middle of the pavement was a standpipe sticking up with a rusty old tap on top. People were queued about ten deep around it, filling all types of containers. Some had bottle carriers, like the ones milkmen used to use, and were filling up plastic bottles. We waited patiently until our turn, and then took only a small plastic bottle full of this precious life giving fluid.

The skeptic in me wondered how a natural spring had so much water pressure, and why the chosen place to have a tap was in the middle of the pavement, but the spiritual part of me, would say that if it makes people feel better to drink this water. Then it is a good thing and hurts no one.

With our miracle water packed we headed for the homeward coach. You would think that the adventure would end there, but that was only the beginning of a new one. The two drivers who had entertained us so well with their cross banter on the outward journey started to show their true colours.

The truth was that they disliked each other intensely, and as the week went on, each tried to gain the support of our group against the other.

Once we were on the road home the atmosphere in the coach became cold. Snide comments were made by the resting driver, as we got lost for a few minutes in Rome. This was followed by a lack of available lira when we got to the first tollbooth. Then there was an argument when the first driver wanted a rest and the second wouldn't take over. In the middle of the night the changing of the radio station awaked us. As each driver kept retuning the radio at five-minute intervals, making some comment like " I can't listen to that shit anymore".

As we reached Switzerland someone commented on the lights across Lake Geneva, and we all woke up to have a look. Shortly afterwards we stopped in a service station. We had changed up £20 into Guilders, and as Daff went off to get a coffee, I purchased a bag of mini bar bell cheeses and a bottle of orange.

Handing over my money I was given one 5-guilder coin in change, and as I sat with Daff we worked out that my items cost £10 and her coffee cost £5. We didn't do anything else in Switzerland, but I guess I can say I've been there and eaten the dearest Edam in the word.

In the car park we lined up to board the coach. Hearing raised voices I turned to see the two coach drivers trying to have a fistfight, whilst some of the passengers were holding them apart. Eventually they were calmed down and our journey continued.

When we left the coach in Dover, they were still arguing, and stopped only to send a hat round, hoping for tips. I gave them my five guilders, (*which was worth about £5*), as it is unlikely that I will ever be able to afford to go to Switzerland again.

I have never been back to Italy, but I know Daff has. Probably because I wanted to be with my new love, it wasn't a good holiday for me. My mobile phone bill that month was three hundred pounds, I'd existed on pot sludge, and been beaten up by a Renault 5.

But looking back, for £135.00, what a great adventure it was.

Randomn Thoughts

Why is it that every time high street stores sell bigger sizes. I get bigger?
Will a Baby on Board Sticker make me drive more carefully?

Why do Big Issue sellers have better clothes than I do?
Why do mothers push prams before them into the flow of traffic?

Why do parents let their children eat goods in the shop, which have not yet been paid for?
Why do taxi drivers think they own the road?

Why doesn't anyone sit next to me?
Why do old people think it's all right to push into queues and be rude to others?

When was the last time you spoke to a teenager?
Why do people talk louder into mobile phones?

Who invented Bling Bling?

I guess this poem gives me a chance to have a rant and tell some randomn stories.

As a man I have always had a problem admitting that someone else can be right, and I can be wrong. After several years of being trained to look at my own biases and listen to what others are saying. I realise that often perceptions make us see the same thing in different ways.

Many years ago I ran a fairground.

Whilst locking up one night I heard a scream. On turning the corner of the building I came upon a young man who was slamming his fist into the face of a girl.

Without speaking I ran over and pulled the man away from her throwing him to the ground.

As I turned to see if the girl was OK a fist hit me in the mouth. Followed by a stream of abuse telling me to leave the guy alone. My eyes cleared to see that it was the girl who was being punched that had punched me.

I've heard similar stories many times. On that occasion I didn't apologise and just walked off. Today without a doubt I would be arrested for assault.

Was I wrong? I don't know but I hope I would have the courage to do the same thing today and if I made a bad judgement have the grace to admit it.

I've always been a big guy and buying clothes is a problem. Over the years I've found that the biggest size in most shops is always one below mine. Having spoken to many small people who have the same problem at the other end of the scale. I guess sizes have to end somewhere but why just below mine?

Some years ago I noticed that bigger cut clothes were gradually finding their way into the shops. But each time they got bigger. So did I.

Thankfully things are getting better as larger clothes are becoming more readily available. But why do they have to be so much more expencive? And who decides when something is OUT-SIZE? And why do shop assistants have to say very loudly." Sorry we have nothing that big in the shop"? And why are the large sizes only in Black or Grey?

I love babies, especially if they are someone else's. But publicising them by putting a sticker in your car isn't necessary. I value all life so why would I drive any more carefully because there is a baby on board? I don't have a sticker saying " Open can of coke on board" or " Fragile laptop ".

I would love to put a giant sticker in my rear window saying. " Beautiful, Kind, Generous, Faultless, Tactile, Vibrant, Voluptuous, Sexy, Compliant, Wife. On Board. (*That's if I had one*).

It's probably the concept of stickers that I don't like and not the poor innocent baby. Sadly most of the cars displaying the sticker don't actually on close inspection, contain a baby.

I'm sure that The Big Issue dose do a good job. Both in publicising the needs of the homeless and those out of work, and by giving a means of earning money. But sometimes my perception sees these sellers in a different light. Look out for the Big Issue seller in the monologue that follows. You'll also find a Taxi driver, a woman with a baby on board sticker and people talking loudly on mobile phones. This was a true event, which happened to me in about 1996.

The Audition

I was out in the garage mending a car. With my head buried deep in the engine of a Mondeo - the telephone began to ring. Looking at my grease-covered hands and with no rag to wipe them. I decided to let the answer machine take a message. As I worked on, curiosity began to get the better of me and eventually I decided to stop for a cup of tea whilst I listened to the tape.

" Hello Pip. It's Russ here. I've got an audition for you. A beer commercial, day after tomorrow. Can you let me know if you're available"?

Now I live on the south coast and auditions for these jobs are always held in London *(normally Soho)*. Having been divorced for a few years with a young daughter and a hefty mortgage, money was tight to say the least. A trip to London would cost me about £25, which was all I had in the world at that time.

Russ's mum Dolly was in fact my agent and had once said to me (*when I was bitchin about auditions*)

" Well if you don't enter the lottery. You can't win it". I thought for a while and decided to find out a bit more.

I dialled the number for The Dolly Brook Agency and Russell picked up the phone." Hi Russ. It's Pip. Can you tell me a bit more about this audition?"

He explained that the commercial was for Miller Light beer. They were looking for someone to play the Managing Director. Could be multi- episodic and only two people were going.

As I was deciding whether to go or not I remembered the Nike advert that I'd auditioned for a few weeks earlier.

I was on the Victoria train at 9am. Onto the underground by 11.00, one change and a walk across London. There were about fifty other hopefuls waiting. We were each in turn asked to slam our fists on a table. " Thanks a lot we'll be in touch if you have the part ". Was all we were told? I never heard from them again. I can't help wondering why I didn't get it? What was wrong with my fist? . I guess I'll never know, but that chance cost me a day in time and £25.

I made my decision." I'll be there Russ. Just let me know the place and time ". He promised to call me by 5pm the next day.

Not knowing the time of the audition I had to make arrangements for my daughter to be collected from school and looked after until I got back. Which could be any time up to 9 pm. My biggest problem was that I'd promised to give my ex wife £25 a week for four years. As a matter of pride I never missed a payment, but with my only £25 ready to finance the audition. I realised I may have a problem this week.

Russ was late with the call and left a message on the answer machine. " Hi Pip. Russ here. The Audition is at 33 Percy Street 2.00 pm Tomorrow. Good luck ".

It was June and the weather was lovely. Knowing that Casting Directors normally have about as much imagination as a fish (*which has a three second attention span*). I put on my pinstriped suit, white shirt and blue tie.

Squeezing into my 1973 Mini Metro I set off for Chichester Railway Station.

On arrival I found that the parking had gone up to

£1-50 a day. After fighting with the sticky label, which stuck everywhere except to the windscreen, I queued up to buy my ticket.

I asked for " A day return to Victoria with the underground on it Please". The ticket woman didn't answer and with a dead pan face pressed some buttons and my ticket was printed out. Pushing it under the bulletproof glass, which separated us, she said "Seventeen Pounds and Sixty Pence". With the money exchanged in silence I headed off for the platform jingling the change I had left. One more stop at the news kiosk and with Chat magazine in hand I took a seat on the bench at the far end of the platform. With ten minutes before the train was due, the platform started to fill up.

A swarthy woman with a large case came and stood next to the one empty seat, which happened to be next to me. She shuffled about for a few moments deciding whether or not to sit down and then walked off dragging her case behind. Another of those unanswered questions formed in my head. " Why's there always an empty seat next to me? Do I smell? Before I could think about it any more, the 9.25 to Victoria pulled into the station.

Having spent many hours in queues for food on film sets, Supermarkets, and theme parks, I just couldn't be bothered to push and shove. So after watching everyone climb onto the train, I boarded closed the door. Walking the full length of five carriages I finally found a seat at the front of the sixth opposite the door.

I put my small bag onto the seat next to me and noticed a young man on the other side of the isle giving me a strange look.

He then stood up and slammed the door shut, which I now realise I had left open. I should have apologised but he wouldn't have heard me as he was wearing a Walkman, which was turned up so loud I could hear the thump of the bass.

What a contrasting pair we must have looked to those who came through the door at regular intervals. The young lad clad in black cycling shorts and pink vest top, whilst I wore a heavy pin stripe suit and was reading a copy of Chat magazine. Thinking about it I was probably the odd one out, on this hot and humid June day.

Out of the next nine people walking through, four left the door open. Each time the young lad would get up and slam it shut harder, looking directly at me as he turned to sit down. (*Perhaps that was my guilty conscience*).

I decided to have a go at the crosswords in my magazine, but after filling in about three answers my pen ran out. Into man mode I went, and taking the pen apart in order to suck the last remaining drops of ink down the cartridge, I dropped the spring onto the floor and spent the next thirty seconds chasing it around with my foot.

Eventually spring retrieved, I put the pen back together but as you would expect it still didn't work. So putting it and the magazine down I decided to think about the Audition.

In his last message Russ had told me that they wanted an American accent. I'd watched a couple of videos the night before trying to take extra notice of the accents and as I sat with my eyes closed I imagined what they would like me to say. " Pour me a Miller". " Miller Light. It must be good - I drink it myself".

After a few minutes I got bored with that and decide to get out the sandwiches, which I'd made before leaving home. Putting my can of coke on the small ledge by my window. I notice that I did in fact have some thing in common with the young man opposite; as he changes his CD and pulled out his home made lunch.

Having finished mine and successfully squeezed all of the wrapping through the hole in the top of my empty drink can, I placed it back on the shelf and settled down to read my magazine. Only to be roused by the crashing of a trolley being propelled through the door by a spotty youth pronouncing. " Track Snax. Sandwiches. Crisps. Tea. Coffee. Soft drinks".

He moved on so quickly that even if I'd wanted something, he would have been gone before I could speak.

Looking out of the window I could see spots of rain against the glass, and then a sudden downpour. For the first time that day, I felt comfortable in my suit as the coolness of the atomised water in the air refreshed the stuffy carriage. Someone behind said to their companion." O what a shame. All those people at Wimbledon will get soaked". Not being a fan of any human sport, I wondered what happens if it rains for a long time? Does Wimbledon fortnight go on for three weeks? Does everyone get their ticket money back? How do they decide who has won?

Before I could form a hypothesis the man with the trolley came crashing back, stopping to pick up the wrappings left by travellers who had consumed his products. As he came level with the cyclist and myself he pulled his black sack back into his stomach in some defiant gesture.

Leaving our homegrown rubbish, he smashed his trolley through the door, which once again was left open. I got up and closed it this time.

There was still a few drops of rain in the air as we pulled into Victoria station and before the train had stopped my cyclist companion was staggering through the carriage door. By the time I stepped onto the platform. He had recovered his racing bike from the guard's van and was pushing it ahead of me. Again I had to wonder "Where is he going to race his bike in Victoria"?

You may have noticed by now that on days out in London I become something of a people watcher. The culture of these City dwellers is so different to that of my own.

As I walked towards the crowd gathering at the platform gate I was overtaken by a small group of stick thin French girls in black pencil skirts (Their language and movement seemed somewhat erotic to me).

We disgorged onto the station and I made my way to the underground. Fighting my way down two flights of stairs. Whilst being beaten by the briefcases and bags of those coming the other way. I finally found the Circle line. After checking I was on the North bound platform, I waited standing close to the wall. I became aware of a man standing unnaturally close to me, looking at the wall behind. For a moment I imagined him to be a mugger or drunk, but then I saw from the corner of my eye a Chocolate machine bolted to the wall behind me. I shuffled along a bit allowing the man to put in his money and collect a small bar of chocolate. Politely he said " Thanks mate" and moved on.

Feeling a gust of wind exiting the tunnel I could hear the approaching train. Whilst I watched the people cram onto the platform (many of which stood beyond the white safety line). The train stopped without anyone falling under it and as the doors opened the fight to get on began. For a moment I forgot where I was and hesitated a bit too long. The doors closed and the train pulled away leaving me almost alone on the platform. Ironically another train arrived about two minutes later and was almost empty.

Taking a seat near the door I began to look at the other people dotted around the carriage. Some were hidden behind newspapers. The Times, The Guardian, The independent. All with front pages on show but the faces of the readers hidden. I only travelled two stations and left at the Embankment to seek out north bound platform three.

My next train contained mainly bureaucratic types. Pinstriped suits and conservative dress. Two smart women were sitting about two seats up showing each other their latest purchases of make up and perfume. A bit further down I noticed a thirty something man standing in the isle, with a briefcase in one hand and a Magnum ice cream in the other. I wished I'd had the sense to buy one and in my jealousy hoped the train would stop sharply and he'd drop it.

Suddenly it dawned on me that being so close to Westminster, there was a good chance these people were the faceless bureaucrats who support those who govern our country. One more stop for me, now I was alone in the carriage with the two sloan rangers and their cosmetics.

Leaving the train at Tottenham Court Road I followed the exit signs and become aware of a growing hoard of people behind me.

All hustling to get to the street as quickly as possible. I made a decision: Not to be intimidated into walking faster, and the crowd washed past me like a wave crashing around a breakwater.

My arms were knocked in different directions as bags and cases bounced off them. Both shins took a beating too. Then finally someone pulling a case on wheels smashed it into my heel and carried on without so much as a " Sorry ". At last I reached the escalator. Surely here I would be safe.

Standing to the right as the machine creaked its way upward. Younger and fitter travellers began to run up the left hand side, still banging bags and laptops into me.

Emerging into the humid City air I stood against a wall and looked around to get my bearings. Although I had an A-Z in my bag. I didn't want to look like a mug tourist. So taking an educated guess I headed off towards what I thought was Percy Street. I must have looked like a local because a lost girl asked me " Can you tell me where Barclays bank is"? I had to apologise and say I was only visiting London.

I don't wear jewellery when I'm in London after an incident in Waterloo station when beggars argued with me after I said I had no change. They pointed at my gold rings and said, "Well give us one of them".

I don't know if my decision not to carry valuables in London, was in order to avoid confrontation or out of fear. Thinking about that incident I became aware of a lack of beggars around me. I hadn't been accosted for money at all yet and it was 11-30 am.

As I walked with purpose I was awakened from my daydream by loud voices. There in the centre of the road, was a Taxi driver shouting abuse across the passenger seat at a woman in an old VW.

She was in the inside lane trying to move out.

As the two moved slowly forward, the woman looked up just in time to skid to a halt before running into the back of a parked window cleaner's van. At which the Taxi driver laughed loudly. Stuck up one finger and accelerated away. Leaving the woman (Who is now well and truly stuck in her lane) to leap from the car and hurl abuse at the window cleaner. Whose lack of interest seems to infuriate her.

Horns began to blow as the traffic behind came to a halt, and as a multitude of raised voices erupted I realise that my interest in the incident has made me miss the turning to percy street, and so I retraced my steps leaving the motorists behind me.

Taking a swift look at my map I turned off the main street and suddenly I was in a much quieter area. No cars just pedestrians, Coffee bars, a' la carte lunches and a cornucopia of greenery.

In a flash it was as if I'd been transported to the Rambles in Barcelona. With over two hours before my audition I found a coffee bar and ordered a Cappuccino. Handing over £1-50 of the loose change in my pocket I sat on a stall by the window and watched the world go by.

Coming from Bognor Regis, London fashion was something of an eye opener for me. My eye was drawn to a young woman walking past. She had long black hair with a white streak to the front left. Her eyes bore heavy black make up and silver studs in her lip, nose and ears reflected the suns rays.

Her long thin black skirt seemed to flair at the bottom like a raged fish tail, whilst the top of her black bra protruded from a low cut white top.

Fingerless black fish net gloves which stood out 3D like against her pale white skin made me think she must have been in the Rocky Horror Show or The Adams Family, but my daughter told me later she was something called a GOTH.

As she disappeared into the distance the sunlight seemed to dim, within seconds the humidity grew and with a crash of thunder, droplets of rain started to hit the window. A woman in a leopard skin mini skirt broke into a run as the ensuing downpour covered her as if a bucket of water had been emptied directly upon her head. As she came level with my view her white silk top was almost transparent.

Her copper bobbed hair was flat and dank. And her nipples stood out like Victorian light switches. I chastised myself for noticing that but my excuse is that it's God's fault.

(He gave men the handicap of Auto Compulsory Nipple Gazing).

Waiting until the cloudburst had finished I left the café and walked the final five hundred yards to 33 Percy Street. Here I was at last ready for my audition Walking up the steps I pressed the button on the intercom. No voice asked what I wanted; just a loud clunk and the door opened an inch.

Pushing it fully open I entered the large hallway and stood alone wondering where to go. Thumping footsteps preceded the arrival of a young man from the bowels of the building. " Hi – You here for the Miller Light Ad?" He asked. " Yep. Pip Frederick from Dolly Brooks" I answered.

191

He then handed me a piece of A4 paper and told me to " Take a seat in the Green Room and fill this out". Strangely enough the "Green Room" is rarely green. It's a generic term for a waiting room used by Actors or in this case wanabees.

The area itself was very much like a Dentists waiting room, sparsely decorated with about nine assorted chairs dotted about. I was still thirty minutes early so I sat down and began to fill in the form. Before I could write much more than my name a voice says " Hello Pip. You here for the Miller light?" Looking up I see it's a guy I've been against in several auditions. He too is wearing a suit and looks surprisingly similar to me.

Before I can ask if he's the other candidate from Dolly's agency, three more suit-clad men appear. It turns out that there are two people coming from every agency in London. Each time I looked up from filling in my form a few more people had entered the room. I couldn't help being a little annoyed at having to fill in all the details that my agent had already supplied, but as I put in my height, weight and colour of hair, I became aware that the room was almost full and those arriving now were of an entirely different category and wearing casual clothes.

Just as I realised the audition was for several different parts I heard the young assistant say to a newcomer " Take a seat. We're running a bit late. You may have to wait about an hour". Turning to me he asked" Can you stand up so I can take a Polaroid?" With a flash of the camera a blank picture roles from the front of the camera. The young man waved it madly until the picture started to develop.

There I stood red eyed and with damp hair framed against the cell like bars which cover the window.

Why, I wonder, did I bother spending £250 on promo photos for my agent to send out when they take a Polaroid on the day?

He stapled the photo to the top of my form and began to work his way round the room doing the same for all the others.

By this time the chairs were all full, and several young blond, blue eyed, fit guys sat on the floor.

In rushed one such fellow and picking up his shoulder bag loudly told one of the others "I had to jump through a hoop. Punch my way out of a paper bag, and roll across the floor". Before any one can say anything he whisked himself out of the room and through the front door.

Watching his departure through the window I noticed that it was raining again and I hoped that this downpour would reduce the humidity in our over-crowded room.

Joining in with the endless chatter and showbiz story telling made the next forty minutes pass quickly, and as I finish telling of my recent filming with French & Saunders in a graveyard near Torquay, a young woman came in.

" Hi Pip you're next. We tried to get you the other week for Eastenders but you weren't available". As I followed the girl down into the basement I remembered who she was.

A year or so earlier I had been working on Casualty in Bristol. I was playing a Greek who had his ear bitten off in a fight. On my first day the blooded bandage was on my left ear. On the second day continuity insisted that it was on my right. After a small debate I was told that. I was only a walk-on and the bandage was put over my right ear. Two days later I was asked to go and retake the scenes because of the mistake. On arrival I took a bollocking and couldn't be bothered to argue.

The girl leading me down the stairs was responsible for the mistake and I guess had remembered me. I'd been working regularly as an extra in Eastenders and it must have been her who asked for me. My agent Dolly had said it was likely that eventually I would be offered a small part and guess what? She phoned me and said I'd been asked for to play a dustman who would be in several episodes as a character. Sadly I'd taken a job in an advert for the post office and my honour wouldn't let me back out just for more money. The part was given to a guy called Ricky who looked like me. He went on to work with Joe Brand and in fact in a lot of stand up comedy shows. Hey Ho.

My dreams of what might have been were interrupted as I was entered a blacked out room. At the far end was a table with four people sitting behind. I was told to sit on a bar stool with lights shining upon me which completely obliterated my view of the others in the room. A disembodied voice came at me from behind the table. Introducing the Director, Producer, Casting Director, and Designer. (The names of whom I don't remember).

The voice continued" Ok Pip we're going to take a video. When I say action I would like you to tell us your name and any adverts you have been in lately. Then in your own time pick up the can of beer on the table next to you. Open it and take a mouthful. Then look into the camera and say Woof.

Trying to look powerful I introduced myself and began. Picking up the can of beer I held it at chest height, about an arms length in front of me.

Puling back the ring a hiss of escaping air preceded an eruption of foam.

Lifting the can slowly to my lips I took a swig, swallowing with a lusty gulp, I wiped my mouth and said. "Woof".

" Great stuff " Says a voice from the darkness. " Now can you do it again in an American accent". WHAT? I can't believe what I've just heard. How the F…k do I say woof in an American accent?

Well I'm here now so I'd better try. "3.2.1. Action". I go through the whole routine again ending with" Wooorrrrffff". The next words I heard were " Thanks a lot. We'll be in touch".

Before I knew it I was outside the front door and heading for the tube station.

As I walked down Tottenham Court road, a young man trying to sell the Big Issue accosted me. " Big Issue. Big Issue" He stood directly in my path pushing the magazine at me and glaring straight into my eyes.

As I stared back at him I saw that he was wearing gold earrings, a Fruit of the Loom jumper, Levi jeans and Timberland boots. I wondered how he could afford better clothes than me and I stepped politely round him mumbling, " Sorry got no change".

I hate lying but I just can't be bothered to have the debate.

Looking back I suppose I didn't know his circumstances. But as I walked down the steps into the underground I wondered how hard he'd tried to get work? I'd just spent my last twenty-five quid, been humiliated by a prat who wanted me to say "Woof" in American, and was up against twenty others to win a day or two's work.

Back on the now crowded underground train I felt like a whale in a tin of sardines. Hanging on to a strap dangling from the roof I listened to the conversation of two girls standing either side of me.

" I can't decide whether to leave him or not. He's a nice guy, but he doesn't rock my world. If I leave him I can go and live with my mum and save eight hundred a month on the rent and in a year I can buy that convertible I've always wanted". " Leave him" the other girl replies.

I wonder what Harold Pinter would have made of that conversation?

As I leave the underground at Victoria a man running down the stairs rams his briefcase into my shoulder. Being about 15 stone heavier than him, the case is ripped from his hand and tumbles down the steps to be picked up by its owner as he runs on. No apology or rebuff.

Taking out the last of my change I purchased a can of coke and a bar of chocolate from one of the kiosks before joining the throng of passengers standing in front of the TV monitors, waiting for their train to arrive on the platform.

It wasn't long before my train flashed up on the monitor over platform 19. *Portsmouth Harbour- Front four carriages only for Chichester.*

People started to run for the train. I couldn't understand why, it didn't leave for another ten minutes. I walked past the first ten carriages and climbed in. Once safely seated in an almost unoccupied carriage.

I smiled to my self, wondering how many people would sit in the first four carriages from the barrier.

When in fact it is the last four, which become the first four once the train moves. *(If you see what I mean)*.

My journey was uneventful until two guys got on at Clapham Junction. They sat adjacent to me and their conversation was I think in German.

After a minute or two Gent number one put his hand in his pocket and pulled out a mobile phone. Having dialled a number, I heard another phone ring. Gent number 2 put his hand in his pocket and pulled out his mobile. The two then had a short conversation before switching off.

Man number 2 then dialled a number. Man number 1 answered his phone and the conversation started again. Eventually both phones were switched off and put away, leaving me wondering, "What was that all about?"

The two guys left the train at Gatwick and the carriage began to fill up. So much so that a young woman was forced to sit next to me. Three rows behind I heard a woman ask, " Does this Train go to Southampton"? The reply was somewhat curt " I don't know. I'm only on this train until Chichester". The woman asked again. "But surely you know if this train goes to Southampton?" The reply made me realise that she is talking to the ticket collector." I'll ask the driver when I get to the front".

With that he ploughed on through the carriage checking our tickets and quickly moved on slamming the door behind him. I'm not even going to describe the insignificant little jobsworth. Someone else explained to the woman that if she stayed in this carriage she would get to Portsmouth Harbour and could change there for Southampton.

For the rest of the journey I thought about the events of the day and decided to write them down so that in the future I could look at it and think. " Well I got my £25 worth that day".

Later that night as I went to bed I remembered the bar of chocolate, which was still in my jacket. It hadn't melted and I ate it whilst sitting on the bed wondering how to tell my ex wife I'd spent her money.

As it happened someone called me out on a breakdown early the next morning and guess how much it cost. Yep. £25.

I didn't get the part.

Medieval Nights

The fire burns high in the Baron's hall.
As roasting swine turns slowly on the
rolling spit.
Browning as it basks in the heated
smoke.
Fat drips onto hot glowing coals.
Igniting with a sizzle and a pop.
Causing the flames to leap and hop.
Guests sit chatting behind loaded tables,
As the minstrel plays a jovial tune.
Until silence interrupts, heralding the
Baron's approach to an expectant room.
Power and presence precede his arrival.
Upon which a wave of one hand signals
The beginning of the banquet.
Servants serve, Entertainers sing.
Dancers dance and petticoats swing.
The fire burns high as the swine feeds
the guests.
Its body thinning with every slice at its
chest.
A comical moment of displeasure ensues.
Into the stocks to pay his dues.
The victim is fastened, head and arms
bound.
Food flies towards him hits
then falls to the ground.

Laughter precedes the next volley of
gunge.
Then arms are released as the
punishments done.
Wine flows as ambient chatter
overthrows the formality of the evening.

The fire burns low, the carcase turns
slow,
Where once the flames had licked at a
bountiful feast.
Stools stand empty, as revellers lay upon
the waste strewn tables.
Overdosed on hospitality, they groan
with contentment.

The Baron majestically surveys the
melee.
Smiling at the success of the evening's
swarey.
With a farewell gesture he slides off to
bed.
Where he'll sleep away the excess of the
wine he's been fed.

For tomorrow is another day
And the wine's already on it's way

One day in the eighties my Agent phoned me and asked if I could play Henry V111 at a medieval dinner in a local hotel. Once he had told me that it was worth £150 I quickly agreed, and armed with a badly made costume, some close up magic tricks and modelling balloons I set off to the Arundel Park Hotel where I entertained the dinner guests accompanied by a minstrel playing a ukulele.

To my amazement the agent got good reports and so began my short career as Henry V111.The minstrel did not do so well and I never saw him again,

Seeing the opportunity for a new show I enhanced my act by adding Head Chopper and Swords Through illusions and the most popular addition was a game I invented called *Donking*.

The props for this game were made from two pairs of tights. One black. One white. Five tennis balls and some card and string.

All of the legs were cut off the tights. Each had a tennis ball pushed into the toe, and a piece of card stapled into the thigh end. By adding a piece of string, which tied around the waist. The *Donkers* were complete. They came in four basic forms; White or Black. Tuck-in or Strap on.

Two women and two men would be chosen as contestants, and after being given names like; Sir Never Hard, and Lady Loose Knickers, they would strap on or tuck in the Donker of their choice - Whilst I commentated with an appropriately near the knuckle dialogue.

Once adjusted so that the *Donker* was about one inch from the floor, they would swing their hips and as the donker became a pendulum. They would try to hit a tennis ball, which had been placed in front of them.

Knocking it the length of the room and between the legs of a chair. Contestants would play two at a time and the winners would then be tied together facing each other and with a Double Donker between their legs, try to knock the ball in opposite directions. (*You had to be there*)

A local brewery took the show up as a recommended theme night, and work started to come in on a regular basis. With a fee of £250 a night I brought in my nephew Dodge to play a new character called Chopper. He became my henchman and stood beside me in silence, ushering the clients to the Stocks when necessary.

Dressed in a full-length black cloak and hood, He was an immediate success with the women, who spent most of the night trying to get him to speak or take off his hood off.

I have to say Dodge, like all the men in our family is extremely faithful and loyal to his wife. He spent most of the time worrying about how she would perceive our show. Any way his job was to install those who offended me in the Stocks so that the other dinners could throw food at them. Or to take the victim outside and crack a whip, whilst encouraging them to scream. Each individual medieval night would leave us with a number of stories to tell. So my first is from the Ship and Bell public house.

The upstairs restaurant only seated about forty people. The Owner had put on a veritable feast and made all of the staff dress up. I knew it was going to be a good night when a buxom lady of some age placed her left breast in my hand and said " You don't get many of them to the pound do you Love ".

Once all the guests were seated I made my usual opening:

"Good evening my Lords and Ladies. Welcome to my banquet. I hope you will all have a wonderful time with me tonight. There are just one or two rules. Gentlemen. If you have any problems with your ladies I'm sure you are all aware that I have an easy and terminal way of dealing with them! Ladies. If your man cannot satisfy you, let me know and I will change him for another, or see to you myself".

I'd then explain that Cigarettes, Forks, and Lager had not been invented yet, and would proceed to remove any that were on show. After showing the stocks and introducing Chopper, the soup would be brought in. On this particular night one bright man shouted out " Excuse me my Lord. My wife's from Australia". Well as that hadn't been found yet I had her locked in a cupboard. Sadly I forgot about her and Choppers attempts to remind me (*without speaking*) went unnoticed. Some 25 minutes later when the lady's husband sheepishly asked " Can I have my wife back please?" I remembered and had Chopper retrieve her. She seemed quite happy about the incident and for the rest of the evening when I said, "Jump" she answered " How high?"

Now the lady who had introduced herself so unforgettably at the beginning of the evening continued to heckle, and consume large amounts of mead. So she eventually had to be taken out and flogged several times during the evening. Sadly the Landlord chose her to take down to introduce to the dinners in the downstairs bar and much later that night he told me what happened.

About half way through the evening we had our *Donking* competition and after cutting off someone's head and performing both illusions and close up magic the evening drew to a close two hours later than advertised. Being deemed a success the Landlord asked us to stay on and have a drink whilst he looked for dates to rebook us. As our small group of lockins sat chatting he told us this story:

The Lady who had shown such passion for the character of Wench, was brought down to encourage those in the downstairs bar to book for the next medieval night. She was only to keen to play up to the middle class suit clad gentlemen who were dinning accompanied by their wifes. Apparently no one even took offence when she bared her breast and offered the gentlemen to" have a suck on this". But when she pulled up her skirt, placing one foot on a man's knee saying " Ere love. Look No Chastity Belt or Knickers". The man's wife could take no more. Slapping both her husband's and the woman's faces she stormed out, leaving the stunned man to wonder what he had done.

The landlord said it was worth giving them their meal free because twelve other people asked when the next medieval night was going to be. The last I saw of the lady concerned she was staggering still in costume towards Hayling Island singing " Show me the way to go home ".

If I had to pick one outrageous night to talk about, it would have to be a pub we worked at in Havant. Our reputation was spreading and each new venue expected me to be even more outrageous than the last. We even had a small following of people who seemed to turn up where ever we went.

We'd done nights where everyone turned up in just his or her underwear with medieval hats. Nights where whole chickens were stuffed down men's trousers whilst they were in the stocks. Soup overheads, and even a night for Bognor Rugby club held in the British legion in Wittering. Where the waitreses walked topless carrying hot fowl as the men groped them and threw the food at each other.

At one point I ducked just in time to let a full 14-inch pate' pass me like a giant flying slug. Only to splat into the new velvet curtains and fall like a cowpat to the floor.

Luckily for me I was only working for the club and not the person who had organised the night.

Apparently the club steward had a nervous breakdown shortly afterwards and left the area.

But Havant was the best.

The night started much as any. The fifty or so guests, all dressed in costume and with the billiard table covered for protection against flying food. It soon became obvious that this lot were up for anything and just wanted a laugh. So I envoked a new rule.

Each time any person was put into the stocks they had to remove an item of clothing. To those men with brain cell deprivation this was a good way of getting naked as quickly as possible. Not only the men but also most of the women ended up spending multiple visits to the stocks.

One guy dressed as Friar Tuck ended up in the stocks with only his scull cap on, and before I could think of his next forfeit. Someone had inserted a rather large Corn on the Cob up his backside. To this day I don't know if his scream was of agony or ecstasy.

I think by now you will give me the benefit of the doubt when it comes to being a letch or chauvinist, but on this evening my resolve was tested to the limit. When a young woman in her twenties was placed in the stocks backwards. I mean with her backside facing the crowd. Removing her bra before bending over to place her head into the open stocks. Her ample rear covered only by a lace edged pair of silk cammy knickers. The room fell into silence and the men looked wide-eyed knowing exactly what each was thinking. (*I think the woman knew too*). After what seemed like an eternity but was in fact a few seconds. I threw my cloak over her and left her covered for the remainder of her stay in the stocks.

That image stayed with both Dodge and I for years. In fact some time later whilst mending a car in our garage, we found some pornography in the boot of a well-respected client. Looking through the magazine (as you do) we thought we recognised one of the women who was wearing a similar garment to that which impressed us so at that medieval night. Strangely having agreed that it was not the woman we'd met, we were both dumfounded when on returning the car, we realised that the picture in the magazine was in fact the wife of the man who owned the car.

Meanwhile back in Havant our night was coming to an end. Almost all of the guests had consumed so much alcohol that they were completely unaware of their near nakedness. Dodge pulled me into a corner and whispered. " The women are gonna get you and take your clothes off. If I help you they say they'll rip mine off too. What shall I do?" I guess my sense of fair play took over.

After all I was the only one who was still fully dressed. So in character I stood next to the Bar Billiard table and announced " My Good Maidens. It has been brought to my attention that you all wish to see my Crown Jewels. Please remove my clothing carefully and savour the experience".

For many reasons, in my heart I am afraid of women. But the sight of twenty or so semi naked ones rushing towards me fighting to get my clothes off was a new type of fear, which was unlike anything I had ever experienced.

My costume did get ripped, and Dodge had to take off his hood and speak. My ordeal did not however end there. Once fully undressed I was pushed onto the plywood cover of the bar billiard table and the remnants of Swede, Chicken, and fruit were rubbed all over my body. And the answer to the question I'm always asked when recounting that night. NO I didn't get aroused. I was crapping myself.

At about 2am after a shower. Dodge and I sat with the die hards who were still naked apart from one man who had a jester's hat on, and told jokes.

I haven't drunk alcohol since the late seventies but Dodge would end up with several pints in front of him brought by our new friends.

Now at about 3am the jokes were getting bad and I'm going to try and do the impossible by telling you a visual joke that has been re told hundreds of times at our family parties, and it amazes me that anyone laughs at it. But they do.

After spending a very pleasant evening in their local pub. Two Tortoises were staggering home together. A few drops of rain started to fall and one turned to the other with his bottom lip protruding said. " Does your mouth fill up with water when it rains?"

His companion turned towards him and with his top lip protruding said " NOP".

I don't know if you get it but that joke told by a naked jester has stayed with me for over 12 years.

The evening ended about 4am when we put the naked Jester into a taxi. The next day Dodge and I couldn't help wondering how he paid the driver as his wallet and clothes were still in the pub?

Not all of the medieval nights were as badly behaved. We were once booked by the Bosham Gardener's Club. We knew when we read the menu that someone had misbooked the evening. The food on offer was something like: Prawn Cocktail followed by Traditional Roast Beef and Choice of sweet from the desert trolley. The tables were in four rows and laid out with knifes forks and spoons. Dodge and I watched in horror as a predominantly elderly cliental came in wearing blazers and ties. Just five or six lonely costumed people sat at the end of the far table. As I explained the evening I realised that those who could hear me hadn't got a clue what I was talking about. But before I could stop him Dodge had taken away all of the knifes and forks.

Because of course they weren't invented yet. Looks of disbelief followed as he continued by taking away the cigarettes and lighters.

Now with their prawn cocktails in front of them the guests sat politely not knowing how to eat. After an uncomfortable five minutes I had to get Chopper to give back the knifes and forks.

On the meal went with all except the costumed group completely ignoring me. Those few however were joining in and I was doing my best to entertain them. With the meal being served as a normal three-course function, everything was finished by about 9 pm and we still had two hours to fill.

In order to play the *Donking* game I had to go into the public bar and collect the village idiot. He happily played the game and then placed his head into a box, which I pushed fourteen swords through. Once finished with he was placed precariously back on his stool in the bar and probably remembered little of the incident the next day.

Then we were joined by the local Newspaper Reporter, who bowled in, taking charge, (as she does), and set up a few photos. Writing down names she spoke to the costumed guests and then left as quickly as she'd arrived.

The evening for Dodge and I had been distinctly flat. I was so disappointed I worried in case organisers refused to pay us. But pay us they did, and with the usual congratulations and handshakes we made our way home arriving at the sickeningly early time of 11.30pm. In fact we were so early that we stopped in West Street to get some chips.

Thursday morning came and my mother phoned to say " You're in the paper again ".
Leaving the gearbox overhaul we were working on, I went over to the Coop and brought the Observer. There in the middle was a full-page spread, with colour photos and a story about this fantastic medieval night and how great it all was. Dodge and I looked at each other across the newspaper and said, " Where were we that night?"

It's only recently that I realised there is a lesson for me to learn from that story.
I know she won't mind me saying this, but an elderly lady I know came over at a dinner recently and said. " We were looking at some old photo's today and we have one of you as Henry the V111 at a dinner in Bosham. I knew it was you but my husband thought it wasn't. It was a great night wasn't it?"
Perception.
That's what I learned. Just because I have to be loud and brash and break out in a sweat, to be enjoying myself. Others can do the same in a sedate and calm manner.
The fact that the guests didn't know what to expect meant that they could enjoy the evening for what it was and not compared to the others we'd done. I'm sorry now I misjudged them, but I'm glad they had a good time.
My Sagittarian nature meant that after a year or two I felt the show had been over exposed, and I wanted to do something different.
So out came Black Beard The Pirate and Master Bates.

The evening ran the same as the medieval but with different jokes and the illusions were replaced with escapology. *Donking* still worked and a large foam plank was introduced along which those who offended me would be forced to walk blindfolded. As they reached the end Master Bates would spray them with water. One night we went to a pub called The Bird in Hand. The landlord was shocked to see us and had made no special plans for the night. Having been booked by the brewery he had to pay us, so said, " Just do what you can ". Expecting a bad night we put on our costumes and set about playing with the people in the restaurant.

An Irish family were having an eightieth birthday meal for Gran, and welcomed our banter and balloon models. The daughter came over to me and said, " Make mum walk the plank". Somewhat worried in case the elderly birthday girl should fall over and hurt herself. I accused her of some misdemeanour and ordered her to walk the plank.

As she wobbled along I held her hand and on reaching the end of the plank. Master Bates (Dodge) Sprayed water up her skirt. She let out a little scream of delight and said " That's the first time my knickers have been wet for years". We went on to have a great night and each one of the hundred or so people in the pub went home with a balloon model. Even the pool team stopped to play with us.

We were paid grudgingly by the unimpressed Landlord and we sat outside the pub making balloons for the Irish family who left about an hour later with the back seat of the taxi filled with models.

Henry was resurrected a while later for one last TV, job, when I found myself at an audition for someone to play The King in a schools history series for the BBC. I was at the audition with my old mate Charlie the Clown, who was there to audition for Henry V11. Charlie was his double. I had no doubt he would get the part, but I am about 4 inches shorter than the great king and quite a few pounds lighter. Having done all the things asked of me by the young female Casting Director, she finished by saying, " Pip I think you look like him, and I would love to use you. But you're just too funny. We want someone who is fierce and foreboding". " But I can act that bit" I replied. " But we don't know that do we?" she answered.

With nothing to lose I put on my best psychopathic face and dragged her over the table, throwing her to the wall like a rag doll and threatening to rip her head off and piss down her throat". " Is that good enough?" I asked as I brushed her down and half carried her back to her chair. " Yes. Yes. You've got the part". Sadly Charlie never got Henry V11.
My first day on the shoot came, and after spending four hours in make up I was shown to a room on the second floor of the studio, which was in the middle of Acton. Carrying the enormous three-layered costume, which had been hired for me from Angels, I backed into the room still talking to the wardrobe girl. " You strip off and put on the underclothes and I'll be back to sew you into the rest in a few minutes" she said. Once inside I put the costume on the floor and proceeded to remove all of my clothes. Standing completely naked I turned to the rear of the room and was faced with a wall of glass.

There in the street one floor below was a small crowd (*mainly girls*) who were watching my strip and found my realisation of their presence most humorous. As is common with me I went into man mode and left the room quickly, only to find myself now standing naked in the hallway of the studio. Strangely the runners and those around seemed not to find my unclothed presence anything unusual.

The costume girl returned and ushered me back into the room where she helped me dress, without comment.

The sad thing about that job is that it was a buy out and didn't have the normal repeat fee attached. Over 15 years later that history series is as far as I know still being shown each year in schools and I don't get a penny.

Our two-man show was great fun to work, and for a few years we made new friends on a daily basis. Fete took me in another direction and I found myself on the road with a new show The Tiny Top Circus. Both King Henry and Black Beard were recycled to become two new characters Hagrid and Poncho and the illusions sit to this day in my prop store.

The poem? Well its what I imagine a medieval banquet would have been like.

But mine were more fun.

I Almost Made it

I almost made it as a Coalman,
But the public switched to gas.
I almost made it in a racing car,
But I let the others pass.
I almost made it on the radio,
But my voice was just too common.
I almost made it mending motors,
But my own broke down too often.

I almost made it as a Dealer,
But I paid too much for the goods.
I almost made it as an Actor,
But my acting's made of wood.
I almost made it as a boy friend,
But I got side tracked by my mates.
I almost made it as a husband,
But work always made me late.

I almost made it as a lover,
But something good came on TV.
I almost made it as a parent,
But the kids hated me.
I almost made it as a singer,
But my harmonies were cold.
I almost made it on e-bay,
But I bought more than I sold.

I almost made it as a friend,
But I lost touch.
I almost made it as a Fruit Picker,
But I didn't like that much.
I almost made it as an adult,
But the child in me got out.
I almost made it as a son,
But Mum always had to shout.

It sounds like I'm a failure.
But that's not what I am.
I'm just an ordinary,
Common garden,
Fun loving,
Type of MAN.

You may think this poem is about failure, but in fact it's about perception. Over the last few years the stories I've told in this book have been shared many times. I began to wonder if I was living in the past. But as I continue to change occupations, perceptions, and adventures even at the age of 49, I remember the words of an old friend, who told me many years ago; " Whatever else comes and goes. No one can take away the things you've done". In my eyes he was right but I add to that. " You can never relive the past. I believe, when it's over let it go and move on."

Last night I was talking with my daughter and some friends. They think I'm a pretty laid back guy. But in my younger days I was as arrogant as a man can be. At one time long before Sam was born, with no money and debt up to my ears. I swanked around in a Merc and smoked cigars that came in individual aluminium tubes. They called me " The Sleek Otter". (*On account of my black fur collared, full-length coat*).

A new sport called Wind Surfing arrived, and for one summer it was my passion. With me weighing seventeen stone my surfboard was aptly named " Wailer" and at ten feet in length with a six-meter sail I negotiated force five winds with ease.

Eventually I was able to surf from the waters edge and land again hardly getting my feet wet.

So one sunny summer day, with the local seashore packed with holidaying families, I decided that it would be funny to put on a suit and tie, and surf out and back from the beach.

For best effect I chose to do this mid day. To the amazement of those on the beach I achieved a perfect launch and surfed out about five hundred yards.

Not content with this I tacked up and down for about ten minutes, before suddenly the rubber joint that connected the mast to the board snapped, launching the sail and me into the sea.

Having taken a windsurfing certificate, I knew the emergency procedure, and rolled the sail round the mast, which I then laid full length along the board.

With the sail de- rigged I lay on top in my pin stripe suit and began paddling towards the shore. The tide was on the turn and for every yard I went forward I seemed to go two back. Laying almost on the waters surface the movement of the sea was like being thrown about in a storm. After about five minutes of riding this briny roller coaster I felt extremely sick, but being well out of my depth fear of drowning kept me going.

After what seemed like a week of struggling (*But was nearer fifteen minutes*). I was half washed up and half staggered onto the beach. Where I immediately threw up.

Some of those watching clapped and others laughed. I threw my board and sail onto the roof rack and drove off as quickly as possible.

My Dad could never understand why his suit didn't fit him after that, and I never surfed off of West Park again.

I've only told you that story so that you can be sure I never have been, and never will be a saint. Even today I sometimes go into man mode and with every brain cell is telling me "NO STOP!" I continue to obey my genetic programming and do or say something stupid.

Just the other week I was at a dinner, and meeting a lady I hadn't seen for some time I said " Hi you've put on weight". Even as the words came out of my mouth I knew I'd done wrong.

I did however have the sense not to try and make things better, and dig a bigger hole for myself. However I didn't get away with it.

The next day I received an e-mail telling me how much I'd upset her. I thought carefully about my reply, which went something like this. " *Hi. I'm so sorry that I upset you. I think I meant to say you look like life is treating you well but it just came out wrong. I hope you can forgive me and we are still friends*".

Her answer will haunt me for the rest of my life.

" *Hi Pip. Correct reply. Of course we are still friends. I find you psychologically interesting*".

So now along with all my other fears and insecurities I'm a psychological idiosyncrasy.

The philosophical side of me believes however that there is always something good just around the corner. It's just that sometimes we can't see it. But that doesn't mean it isn't there.

Many times I've been scared by the circumstances of my life, but I kept running even when it was into darkness. Always somewhere ahead I've found a light and a new path.

I don't have a religion but I do believe we are here to learn, to experience, and to be human.

Most of all I think I've been human.

True to my gender and in many cases just plain stupid.

I still have much to learn and as I move on into my 50s I have new dreams and adventures to undertake.

If indeed a stranger is just a friend you haven't met,
then it is my greatest wish that our journey through
these pages together has made me a new friend to
you, and I hope you've found the experience
entertaining.
I've laid before you my life, my fears, and my
vulnerability.

Like me or Hate me. I ask only that you
" Forgive me. I'm a man".